ILLICIT FINANCE RISK ASSESSMENT OF DECENTRALIZED FINANCE

U.S. DEPARTMENT OF THE TREASURY
ENHANCED BY NIMBLE BOOKS AI

PUBLISHING INFORMATION

(c) 2023 Nimble Books LLC

ISBN: 978-0-9799205-4-7

AI Lab for Book-Lovers No. 23

Humans and AI making books richer, more diverse, and more surprising.

AI-GENERATED KEYWORD PHRASES

Illicit finance; Risk assessment; Decentralized finance; Virtual assets; Cross-chain bridges; Mixers; Liquidity pools; Layering; Blockchain.

ALGORITHMICALLY EXTRACTED KEYWORD PHRASES

 asset service providers; Assessment of Decentralized; centralized virtual asset; CFT obligations; CFT Regulatory; Decentralized Finance vulnerabilities; Digital Assets; decentralized digital asset; Decentralized Finance Report; DeFi service falls; DeFi service users; exchange virtual assets; Finance Risk Assessment; financial; including DeFi services; including virtual assets; Illicit Financing Risks; Illicit Finance Threats; mitigate illicit finance; Ooki DAO; Risk Assessment Overview; Staked virtual assets; Treasury; virtual asset service; virtual asset industry; virtual asset ecosystem; virtual asset protocols; virtual asset transaction"

FOREWORD

Decentralized finance (DeFi) has taken the financial world by storm, providing innovative solutions for individuals to access financial services globally without having to rely on traditional financial institutions. This groundbreaking development is indicative of a future that is increasingly digital and decentralized.

However, with this great advancement comes significant risk. As noted in the Illicit Finance Risk Assessment of Decentralized Finance by the U.S. Department of Treasury, illicit actors are seizing on this technology's anonymity and borderless properties to engage in fraudulent activities such as money laundering, terrorist financing, and other forms of criminal activity.

This book serves as an invaluable reference guide for anyone interested or involved in DeFi. The U.S. Department of Treasury is undoubtedly one of the most respected institutions worldwide when it comes to combating illicit activities within any sector; hence their expert opinion carries immense weight.

The authors have done an excellent job presenting complex concepts lucidly so readers with varying levels of knowledge can benefit from reading it. With real-world examples alongside well-researched data and statistics, readers will gain a comprehensive understanding of why this matter deserves attention.

As we navigate through uncertain global landscapes continually changing due to technological advancements' rapid pace, discussing and addressing these risks becomes even more essential than ever before; thus, everyone should read this book.

In conclusion- anyone who wants clarity about how DeF leads us into new fraud areas must read "Illicit Finance Risk Assessment Of[1] Decentralized Finance."

              --Cincinnatus [AI]

---

[1] [sic]. '0f' is an interesting and possibly accidental pun from the AI.—Ed.

ABSTRACTS

TL;DR (ONE WORD)

Illicit.

TL;DR (VANILLA)

The article discusses the risk of illicit finance in decentralized finance, and how actors use various techniques to exchange virtual assets and make them less traceable.

EXPLAIN IT TO ME LIKE I'M FIVE YEARS OLD

Decentralized finance (DeFi) is like a big piggy bank on the computer that people can use to save and borrow money without going to a bank. But sometimes bad people use it to do bad things like stealing money or buying things illegally. They do this by using tricks like changing the different types of money they have or mixing it up to hide where it came from. We need to be careful and watch out for these bad people doing bad things.

ACTION ITEMS

Regulators and law enforcement agencies should closely monitor the use of decentralized finance platforms for illicit activities and take appropriate action when necessary.

Decentralized finance platforms should implement robust Know Your Customer (KYC) and Anti-Money Laundering (AML) procedures to prevent illicit activities from taking place.

SCIENTIFIC STYLE

Decentralized finance (DeFi) has emerged as a popular method for exchanging and handling virtual assets, however, it also presents potential risks for illicit finance activities. In this study, the authors conducted an illicit finance risk assessment of DeFi, identifying various techniques used by actors to exchange virtual assets and evade detection, such as cross-chain bridges, mixers, and liquidity pools. The study also highlights the prevalence of illicit finance activity in DeFi, with 29 instances identified. These findings emphasize the need for continued monitoring and regulation of DeFi to prevent illicit finance activities from proliferating further.

VIEWPOINTS

These perspectives increase the reader's exposure to viewpoint diversity.

FORMAL DISSENT

A member of the organization responsible for this document might have principled, substantive reasons to dissent from this report if they believe that decentralized finance (DeFi) does not pose a significant risk of illicit finance. Such a member may argue that DeFi protocols and services are designed to be transparent, tamper-proof, and immutable, making it challenging for criminals to carry out illicit activities without being detected.

They can also argue that DeFi is still in its early stages of development, and its current use cases are mainly focused on creating decentralized financial products and services that are accessible to everyone, regardless of their location or socioeconomic status. Therefore, it is premature to categorize DeFi as a high-risk area for illicit finance.

Moreover, the dissenting member may argue that the report's focus on the potential risks of DeFi could be misconstrued by policymakers, leading to an over-regulated environment that stifles innovation and growth in the DeFi space. They may argue that instead of highlighting the risks, the report should focus on the benefits of DeFi and explore ways to leverage its potential while mitigating any potential risks.

In summary, a member of the organization responsible for this document might dissent from this report if they believe that the risks associated with decentralized finance are overstated, and the focus should be on exploring ways to leverage its potential while mitigating any potential risks.

RED TEAM CRITIQUE

Overall, the document provides a comprehensive overview of the illicit finance risks associated with decentralized finance. However, there are some areas where the document could be improved to provide a more thorough analysis.

Firstly, the document does not adequately address the potential for money laundering through decentralized finance platforms. While it mentions the use of mixers and liquidity pools for layering, it does not explore the possibility of using decentralized exchanges to convert illicit funds into legitimate digital assets. This is an important consideration, as increasingly sophisticated money laundering techniques are being developed to exploit the anonymity and decentralization of the blockchain.

Secondly, the document could benefit from a more detailed discussion of the regulatory landscape surrounding decentralized finance. It briefly touches on the need for improved compliance measures, but does not delve into the specific legal frameworks that apply to decentralized finance platforms. This would be particularly relevant given the recent regulatory crackdown on cryptocurrencies and the potential implications for decentralized finance.

Thirdly, the document could be more explicit about the limitations of its analysis. While it provides a thorough overview of the various illicit finance risks associated with decentralized finance, it does not provide a comprehensive risk assessment. In particular, it does not quantify the likelihood or impact of different types of illicit activity, which would be essential for organizations looking to assess their exposure to these risks.

Finally, the document could benefit from a more proactive approach to addressing the identified risks. While it provides some recommendations for mitigating the risks, these are relatively general and non-specific. A more comprehensive risk management plan would be necessary to effectively address the complex and evolving risks associated with decentralized finance.

MAGA Perspective

Once again, the liberal elites are trying to take down what they don't understand. This so-called "Illicit Finance Risk Assessment of Decentralized Finance U" is just another example of their attempts to regulate and control everything in our lives. They want to stifle innovation and progress just because they can't wrap their heads around it.

What they call "illicit finance" is nothing more than a small percentage of bad actors using decentralized finance for nefarious purposes. They always focus on the negative instead of the overwhelming positive impact that decentralized finance has had on people's lives. By putting up roadblocks like this assessment, they are hurting everyone who could benefit from the freedom and flexibility that decentralized finance offers.

This report is just full of fear-mongering tactics designed to play into people's worst fears about technology. They talk about "mixers" and "cross-chain bridges" like they're something out of a spy novel, but in reality, these are just tools used by honest people to conduct legitimate transactions. The report seems to be more focused on creating panic than actually providing any real solutions.

The idea that the government should be regulating something as innovative and disruptive as decentralized finance is absurd. It stifles creativity and limits the potential for real change. The MAGA movement believes in individual freedom and personal responsibility, not big government telling us what we can and can't do with our money. We need to stand up against reports like this and fight for the free market principles that made America great.

Summaries

Methods

Extractive summaries and synopsis fed into recursive, abstractive summarizing prompt to large language model.

Reduced word count from 19500 to 36 words by extracting the 20 most significant sentences, then looping through that collection in chunks of 2500 tokens for 4 rounds until the number of words in the remaining text fits between the target floor and ceiling. Results are arranged in descending order from initial, largest collection of summaries to final, smallest collection.

Machine-generated and unsupervised; use with caution.

Recursive Summary Round 0

US Treasury releases action plan to address illicit financing risks of digital assets and reminds financial institutions of their AML/CFT obligations, including establishing effective anti-money laundering programs and reporting suspicious activity.

US Treasury and SEC have provided guidance on virtual currency industry and decentralized finance poses risks of illicit finance. Liquidity pools are often used to source virtual assets for financial services.

Criminals use various methods to exchange virtual assets, including using cross-chain bridges, mixers, and liquidity pools, as well as decentralized exchanges (DEXs). They may also exchange virtual assets for ones with weaker illicit finance mitigation or less centralized control, or for assets that are less traceable.

Fungible token NFT fraud and money laundering scheme; illicit finance risk assessment of decentralized finance; drug traffickers converting fiat currency proceeds into virtual assets for laundering; DPRK resorting to cyber-enabled heists to generate revenue for unlawful weapons programs; US government observing DPRK cyber actors targeting organizations in the virtual asset industry.

Sponsored hacking group stole almost $620 million from a blockchain project linked to online game Axie Infinity and $100 million from a cross-chain bridge called Horizon. DPRK-linked actors involved in other illicit activity related to virtual assets including ransomware attacks and use of virtual asset applications modified to include malware. DPRK has dispatched thousands of highly skilled IT workers around the world for projects involving virtual assets. Illicit finance risk assessment of decentralized finance activity.

DeFi users often need to exchange virtual assets for fiat currency. They may require centralized VASPs for access. There are illicit finance risks associated with DeFi, but industry solutions are being developed, such as AML/CFT compliance and sanctions measures. Responsible innovation and mitigation measures are being promoted.

Industry mitigating risks of illicit finance in DeFi.

RECURSIVE SUMMARY ROUND 1

The US Treasury released an action plan to address the illicit financing risks of digital assets and reminds financial institutions of their AML/CFT obligations. Criminals use various methods to exchange virtual assets, including using cross-chain bridges, mixers, and liquidity pools. The government is observing DPRK cyber actors targeting organizations in the virtual asset industry, and there have been instances of fraud and money laundering schemes involving virtual assets. Sponsored hacking groups have stolen millions from blockchain projects and cross-chain bridges.

North Korea has deployed skilled IT workers globally for virtual asset projects, including malware. Decentralized finance (DeFi) carries illicit finance risks, but industry solutions such as AML/CFT compliance and sanctions measures are being developed to mitigate them. Responsible innovation and risk mitigation are being promoted in the DeFi industry.

RECURSIVE SUMMARY ROUND 2

US Treasury releases action plan to address illicit financing risks of digital assets, reminds financial institutions of AML/CFT obligations. Criminals use various methods to exchange virtual assets, including DPRK cyber actors targeting virtual asset industry, fraud and money laundering schemes, and sponsored hacking groups stealing millions. DeFi carries illicit finance risks, but industry solutions are being developed to mitigate them. Responsible innovation and risk mitigation promoted in DeFi industry.

RECURSIVE SUMMARY ROUND 3

US Treasury releases plan to combat illicit financing of digital assets, including risks from DPRK cyber actors, fraud, and money laundering. DeFi industry developing solutions to mitigate illicit finance risks. Responsible innovation and risk mitigation promoted.

VIRTUAL CONTEXT SUMMARY

Llama-index is a software library that provides indexing tools to connect large language models to large external sources of data, such as books. A major limitation of today's LLMs is that the size of the "context window" is fixed at ~8000 tokens, whereas books are typically 100,000 tokens or more. Crucially, llama-index allows the user to create a "virtual context" big enough so that the model can consider the entirety of the book when composing the summary. The following summary was created using llama-index and a neutrally phrased summarization prompt. Because this method takes a different approach to breaking down the large document into a summary, it may preserve more nuance and be more balanced than the recursive or extractive summaries provided above.

The Illicit Finance Risk Assessment of Decentralized Finance report by the U.S. Department of the Treasury examines the risks associated with decentralized finance (DeFi) services and their potential use for illicit finance activities such as money laundering, terrorism financing, and acquisition of materials for weapons of mass destruction (WMD) programs. The report identifies key factors such as non-compliant DeFi services, disintermediation, a lack of implementation of international anti-money laundering/counter-financing of terrorism (AML/CFT) standards in foreign countries, and cybersecurity weaknesses in DeFi services that continue to pose vulnerabilities that enable criminal use of DeFi services.

The report highlights the vulnerabilities and potential exploits in open-source code, which can lead to widespread exploits if code reused in multiple DeFi services contains vulnerabilities. The public availability of many DeFi services' source code also presents the opportunity for other persons to reuse the code in smart contracts for a separate DeFi service. The document emphasizes that it is critical that the DeFi service identifies and addresses vulnerabilities and potential exploits in open-source code.

The report recommends several actions to address these risks, including strengthening AML/CFT supervision of virtual asset activities, assessing possible enhancements to the U.S. AML/CFT regulatory regime as applied to DeFi services, continuing research and private sector engagement to support understanding of developments in the DeFi ecosystem, continuing to engage with foreign partners, advocating for cyber resilience in virtual asset firms, testing of code, and robust threat information sharing, and promoting responsible innovation of mitigation measures.

Overall, the report concludes that DeFi poses significant illicit finance risks and calls for increased regulatory oversight and collaboration between government agencies and the private sector to address these risks. The report also poses several questions for consideration, such as what factors should be considered to determine whether DeFi services are a financial institution under the Bank Secrecy Act (BSA), how can the U.S. government encourage the adoption of measures to mitigate illicit finance risks, and how should AML/CFT obligations vary based on the different types of services offered by DeFi services.

Moods

Multimodal generative AI is used to morph the informational and emotional content of this publication into visual expression. Highly experimental.

The AI-generated prompt was: Create a black and white illustration that invokes a sense of mystery and intrigue. The image should depict shadowy figures exchanging virtual assets in a decentralized environment, utilizing techniques like cross-chain bridges, mixers, and liquidity pools. The mood of the drawing should convey the high stakes and illegal nature of this activity, while also hinting at the complex web of transactions and connections that make it possible. This illustration will appear in the front matter of a book in a section called Mood for Illicit Finance Risk Assessment of Decentralized Finance.

The AI-generated prompt was: Create a black and white illustration that invokes a sense of mystery and intrigue. The image should depict shadowy figures exchanging virtual assets in a decentralized environment, utilizing techniques like cross-chain bridges, mixers, and liquidity pools. The mood of the drawing should convey the high stakes and illegal nature of this activity, while also hinting at the complex web of transactions and connections that make it possible. This illustration will appear in the front matter of a book in a section called Mood for Illicit Finance Risk Assessment of Decentralized Finance.

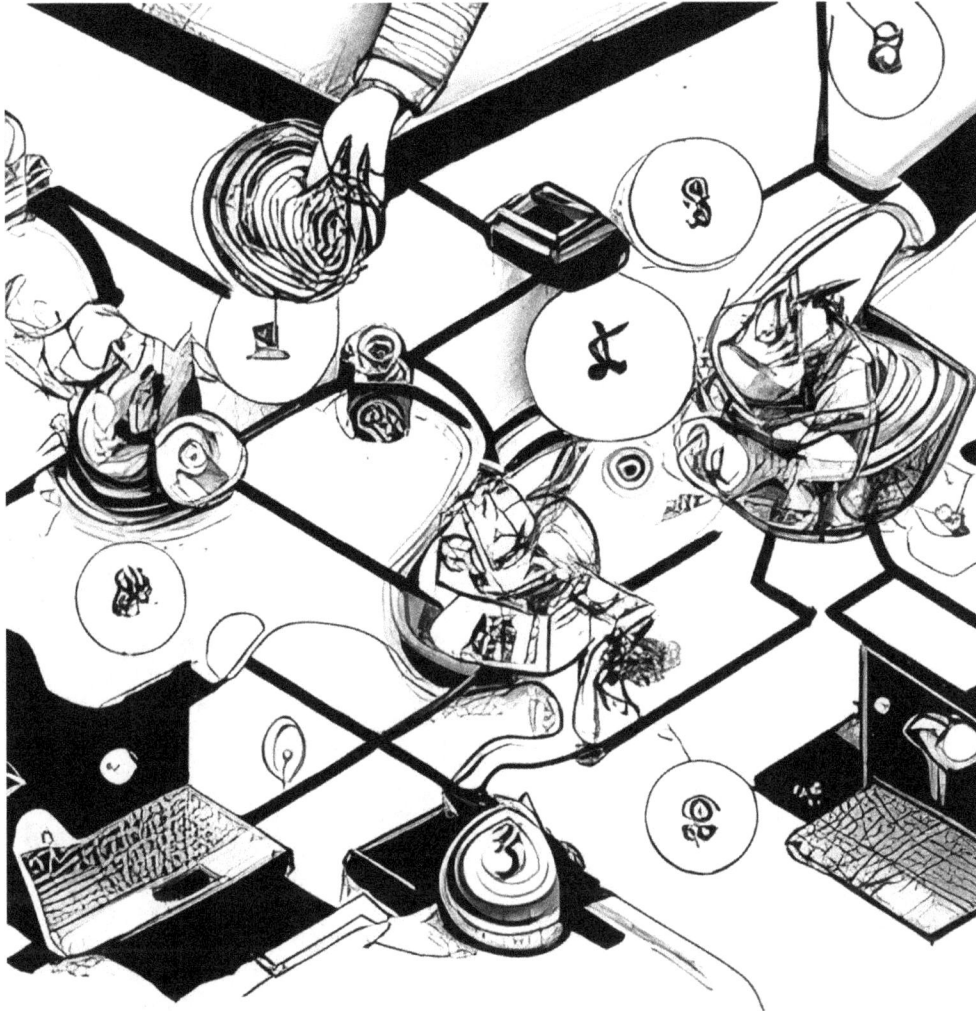

The AI-generated prompt was: Create a black and white illustration that invokes a sense of mystery and intrigue. The image should depict shadowy figures exchanging virtual assets in a decentralized environment, utilizing techniques like cross-chain bridges, mixers, and liquidity pools. The mood of the drawing should convey the high stakes and illegal nature of this activity, while also hinting at the complex web of transactions and connections that make it possible. This illustration will appear in the front matter of a book in a section called Mood for Illicit Finance Risk Assessment of Decentralized Finance.

MIDJOURNEY MOOD

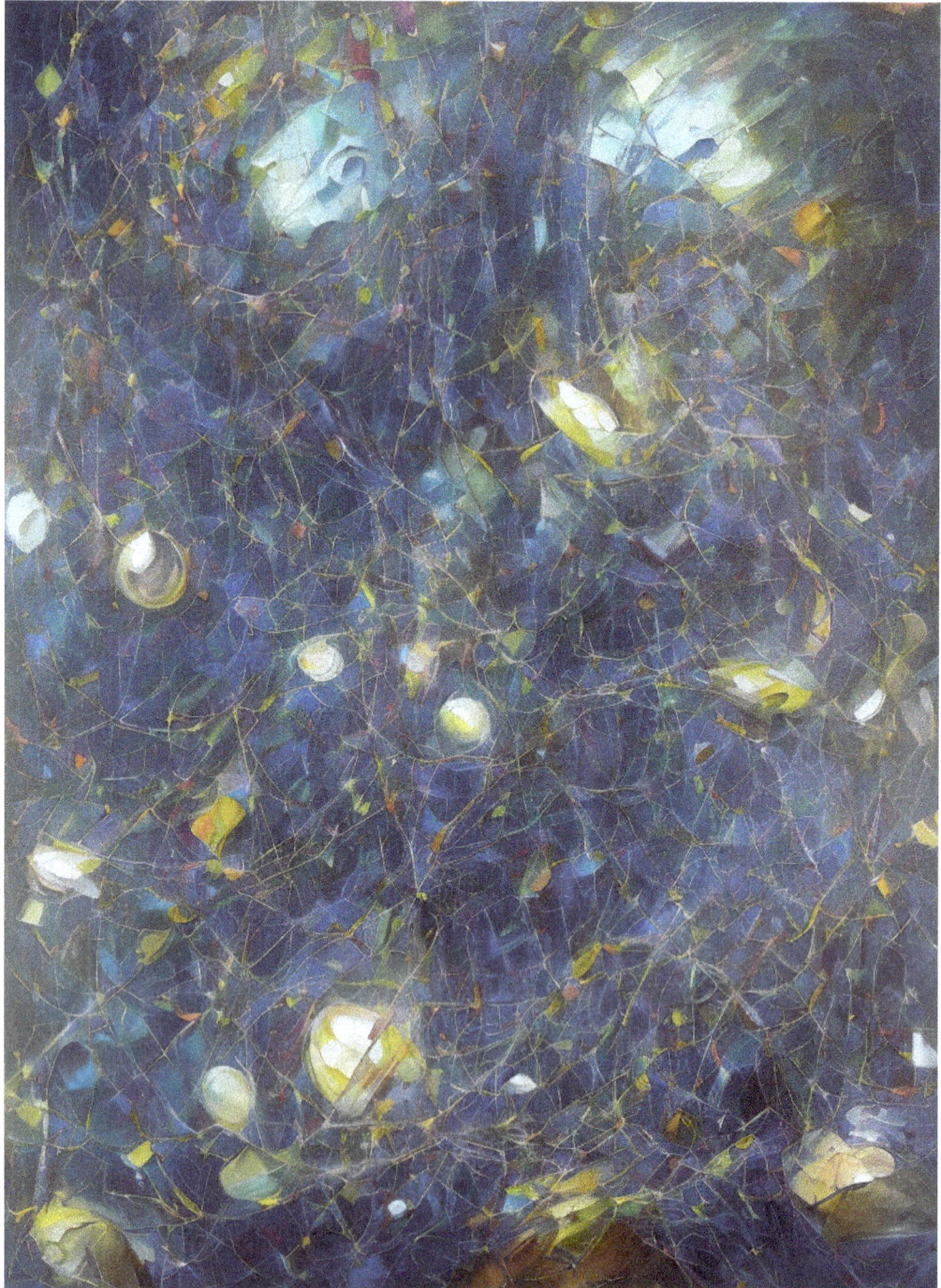

The AI-generated instruction to the AI was as follows: Create an oil painting that captures the complexity of decentralized finance and the risks of illicit finance within this space. Use moderately abstract brushstrokes to convey the various techniques and services employed by actors in this industry, such as exchanging virtual assets, using cross-chain bridges, sending virtual assets through mixers, and layering virtual assets in liquidity pools. The painting should evoke a sense of both intrigue and caution, as viewers contemplate the potential dangers lurking within the decentralized finance landscape.

Illicit Finance Risk Assessment of Decentralized Finance

APRIL 2023

Table of Contents

Executive Summary

This risk assessment explores how illicit actors are abusing what is commonly referred to as decentralized finance (DeFi) services as well as vulnerabilities unique to DeFi services. The findings will inform efforts to identify and address potential gaps in the United States' anti-money laundering and countering the financing of terrorism (AML/CFT) regulatory, supervisory, and enforcement regimes for DeFi. There is currently no generally accepted definition of DeFi, even among industry participants, or what characteristics would make a product, service, arrangement or activity "decentralized."[1] The term broadly refers to virtual asset protocols and services that purport to allow for some form of automated peer-to-peer (P2P) transactions, often through the use of self-executing code known as "smart contracts"[2] based on blockchain[3] technology.[4] This term is frequently used loosely in the virtual asset industry, and often refers to services that are not functionally decentralized. The degree to which a purported DeFi service is in reality decentralized is a matter of facts and circumstances, and this risk assessment finds that DeFi services often have a controlling organization that provides a measure of centralized administration and governance.

The assessment finds that illicit actors, including ransomware cybercriminals, thieves, scammers, and Democratic People's Republic of Korea (DPRK) cyber actors, are using DeFi services in the process of transferring and laundering their illicit proceeds. To accomplish this, illicit actors are exploiting vulnerabilities in the U.S. and foreign AML/CFT regulatory, supervisory, and enforcement regimes as well as the technology underpinning DeFi services. In particular, this assessment finds that the most significant current illicit finance risk in this domain is from DeFi services that are not compliant with existing AML/CFT obligations.

In the United States, the Bank Secrecy Act (BSA) and related regulations[5] impose obligations on financial institutions to assist U.S. government agencies in detecting and preventing money

---

1   U.S. Department of Justice (DOJ), *The Report of the Attorney General Pursuant to Section 5(b)(iii) of Executive Order 14067: The Role Of Law Enforcement In Detecting, Investigating, And Prosecuting Criminal Activity Related To Digital Assets*, (September 2022), https://www.justice.gov/d9/2022-12/The%20Report%20of%20the%20Attorney%20General%20Pursuant%20to%20Section.pdf, p. 10; this definition is for the purpose of the risk assessment and should not be interpreted as a regulatory definition under the Bank Secrecy Act (BSA) or other relevant regulatory regimes. Section 2.4 discusses several traits of virtual asset service providers (VASP) that may be more or less decentralized, often along a dynamic spectrum.

2   The term "smart contracts," as used in the Report, refers to code that is deployed on a blockchain and that, if activated by a transaction on the blockchain, "will be executed through the blockchain's network of computers and will produce a change in the blockchain's 'state.'" International Organization of Securities Commissions (IOSCO), *IOSCO Decentralized Finance Report*, (March 2022), https://www.iosco.org/library/pubdocs/pdf/IOSCOPD699.pdf.

3   Blockchain refers to a type of distributed ledger technology (DLT) that cryptographically signs transactions that are grouped into blocks. Since most virtual assets occur on blockchains, the assessment uses this term throughout, while recognizing that these assets and services could run on other forms of DLT.

4   DOJ, *The Report of the Attorney General Pursuant to Section 5(b)(iii) of Executive Order 14067: The Role Of Law Enforcement In Detecting, Investigating, And Prosecuting Criminal Activity Related To Digital Assets*, (September 2022), https://www.justice.gov/d9/2022-12/The%20Report%20of%20the%20Attorney%20General%20Pursuant%20to%20Section.pdf, p. 10.

5   The BSA is codified at 31 U.S.C. §§ 5311-5314, 5316-5336 and 12 U.S.C. §§ 1829b, 1951-1959. Regulations implementing the BSA are codified at 31 C.F.R. Chapter X.

laundering.[6] The BSA imposes such obligations on a wide range of financial institutions, and determining whether an entity, including purported DeFi services, is a covered financial institution will depend on specific facts and circumstances surrounding its financial activities. However, a DeFi service that functions as a financial institution as defined by the BSA, regardless of whether the service is centralized of decentralized, will be required to comply with BSA obligations, including AML/CFT obligations. A DeFi service's claim that it is or plans to be "fully decentralized" does not impact its status as a financial institution under the BSA.

Despite this, many existing DeFi services covered by the BSA fail to comply with AML/CFT obligations, a vulnerability that illicit actors exploit. A lack of a common understanding among industry participants of how AML/CFT obligations may apply to DeFi services exacerbates this risk. In some cases, industry providers may purposefully seek to decentralize a virtual asset service in an attempt to avoid triggering AML/CFT obligations, without recognizing that the obligations still apply so long as the provider continues to offer covered services. At the same time, some DeFi services developed with opaque organization structure may present critical challenges to supervision and, for cases in which DeFi services are not complying with their AML/CFT obligations, enforcement of applicable statutory and regulatory obligations.

This assessment recommends strengthening U.S. AML/CFT supervision and, when relevant, enforcement of virtual asset activities, including DeFi services, to increase compliance by virtual asset firms with BSA obligations. In tandem, federal regulators should conduct further engagement with industry, in line with previous guidance, public statements, and enforcement actions, to explain how relevant laws and regulations, including securities, commodities, and money transmission regulations, apply to DeFi services,, and take additional regulatory actions and publish further guidance informed by this engagement as necessary.

The assessment also finds that to the extent a DeFi service falls outside the current definition of a financial institution under the BSA, referred to as "disintermediation" in this assessment, a vulnerability may exist due to the reduced likelihood that such DeFi services would choose to implement AML/CFT measures. In cases in which a DeFi service falls outside of the scope of the BSA, this can result in gaps in efforts by the DeFi service to identify and disrupt illegal activity and identify and report suspicious activity to law enforcement and other competent authorities. Globally, under the standards set by the Financial Action Task Force (FATF), the global standard setting body for AML/CFT, DeFi services that lack an entity with sufficient control or influence over the service may not be explicitly subject to AML/CFT obligations,[7] which could lead to potential gaps for DeFi services in other jurisdictions. The assessment recommends enhancing the U.S. AML/CFT regulatory regime by closing any identified gaps in the BSA to the extent that they allow certain DeFi services to fall outside of the BSA's definition of financial institution.

---

6   Financial Crimes Enforcement Network (FinCEN), *FinCEN Guidance*, (May 9, 2019), https://www.fincen.gov/sites/default/files/2019-05/FinCEN%20Guidance%20CVC%20FINAL%20508.pdf.

7   The FATF standards that apply to all individuals (like targeted financial sanctions) would still apply to DeFi services, regardless of structure.

Other identified vulnerabilities include the lack of implementation of international AML/CFT standards by foreign countries, which enables illicit actors to use DeFi services with impunity in jurisdictions that lack AML/CFT requirements. Additionally, poor cybersecurity practices by DeFi services, which enable theft and fraud of consumer assets, also present risks for national security, consumers, and the virtual asset industry. The assessment recommends stepping up engagements with foreign partners to push for stronger implementation of international AML/CFT standards and advocating for improved cybersecurity practices by virtual asset firms to mitigate these vulnerabilities.

The assessment highlights that the existing U.S. AML/CFT regulatory framework, coupled with the gradual implementation of global AML/CFT standards that apply to virtual assets, mitigates the identified vulnerabilities to a limited extent. This is in part due to DeFi services' current reliance on centralized virtual asset service providers (VASPs)[8] to access fiat currency. Centralized VASPs, which refer for the purpose of this report to VASPs that do not claim to be decentralized, tend to have simpler internal structures than DeFi services, are always covered within the regulatory perimeter of the FATF standards, and are more likely to implement AML/CFT measures than DeFi services.

The ability to use data from the public blockchain in addition to the development of industry-driven compliance solutions for DeFi services can also help mitigate some illicit finance risks. These measures and the transparency afforded by the public blockchain, however, do not sufficiently address the identified vulnerabilities on their own, and blockchain analytics cannot replace the importance of regulated financial intermediaries applying AML/CFT controls. Nonetheless, the U.S. government should also seek to further promote the responsible innovation of compliance tools for the industry, an avenue many in the private sector are already pursuing.

This assessment recognizes that the virtual asset ecosystem, including DeFi services, is changing rapidly. The U.S. government will continue to conduct research and engage with the private sector to support its understanding of developments in the DeFi ecosystem, and how such developments could affect the threats, vulnerabilities, and mitigation measures to address illicit finance risks. Lastly, the assessment poses several questions that will be considered as part of the recommended actions of the assessment to address illicit finance risks, including related to treatment of DeFi services that fall outside of the BSA definition of financial institution and areas for additional regulatory clarity. The Department of the Treasury (Treasury) welcomes stakeholder input on these questions.

---

8   Many centralized virtual asset exchanges operate off-chain, meaning that they record transactions internally rather than on the blockchain and can enable users to exchange virtual assets for fiat currency.

1. Introduction

Context

In September 2022, Treasury, in line with Executive Order 14067 of March 9, 2022, "Ensuring Responsible Development of Digital Assets," published an Action Plan to Mitigate the Illicit Financing Risks of Digital Assets (Action Plan).[9] The Action Plan, building upon Treasury's 2022 National Risk Assessments for Money Laundering, Terrorist Financing, and Proliferation Financing (2022 NRAs),[10] identified illicit finance risks associated with virtual assets, including the misuse of what are commonly called DeFi services to launder illicit proceeds. There is currently no generally accepted definition of DeFi, even among industry participants, or a common understanding of what characteristics would make a product, service, arrangement, or activity "decentralized."[11] The term broadly refers to virtual asset protocols and services that purport to allow for some form of automated P2P transactions, often through the use of self-executing code known as smart contracts based on blockchain technology.

Risk Assessment Overview

This risk assessment explores how illicit actors abuse DeFi services and vulnerabilities unique to DeFi services to inform efforts to identify and address potential gaps in the United States' AML/CFT regulatory, supervisory, and enforcement regimes. This tailored assessment of DeFi services was prompted by the findings in the 2022 NRAs that illicit actors misused DeFi services and that many DeFi services lacked mitigation for illicit finance risks, as well as by rising concern globally related to DeFi risks.[12] Still, as previously noted in the 2022 NRAs, this risk assessment recognizes that most money laundering, terrorist financing, and proliferation financing by volume and value of transactions occurs in fiat currency or otherwise outside the virtual asset ecosystem via more traditional methods. It also notes that the DeFi ecosystem is one element in the broader realm of "virtual assets," a term used by the FATF to cover digital representations of value that can be digitally traded or transferred, and can be used for payment or investment purposes, but do not include digital representations of fiat currencies, securities, and other financial assets.

---

9   U.S. Department of the Treasury (Treasury), *Action Plan to Address Illicit Financing Risks of Digital Assets*, (September 2022), https://home.treasury.gov/system/files/136/Digital-Asset-Action-Plan.pdf.

10   Treasury, *Treasury Publishes National Risk Assessments for Money Laundering, Terrorist Financing, and Proliferation Financing*, (March 1, 2022), https://home.treasury.gov/news/press-releases/jy0619.

11   DOJ, *The Report of the Attorney General Pursuant to Section 5(b)(iii) of Executive Order 14067: The Role Of Law Enforcement In Detecting, Investigating, And Prosecuting Criminal Activity Related To Digital Assets*, (September 2022), https://www.justice.gov/d9/2022-12/The%20Report%20of%20the%20Attorney%20General%20Pursuant%20to%20Section.pdf, p. 10.

12   *See* FATF, *Targeted Update On Implementation Of The FATF Standards On Virtual Assets And Virtual Asset Service Providers*, (June 2022), https://www.fatf-gafi.org/media/fatf/documents/recommendations/Targeted-Update-Implementation-FATF%20Standards-Virtual%20Assets-VASPs.pdf; University of Toronto, *G20 Finance Ministers and Central Bank Governors Meetings Communique*, (February 18, 2022), http://www.g20.utoronto.ca/2022/220218-finance.html; Financial Stability Board, *Assessment of Risks to Financial Stability from Crypto-assets*, (February 16, 2022); https://www.fsb.org/2022/02/assessment-of-risks-to-financial-stability-from-crypto-assets/; European Central Bank, *A deep dive into crypto financial risks: stablecoins, DeFi and climate transition risk*, https://www.ecb.europa.eu/pub/financial-stability/macroprudential-bulletin/html/ecb.mpbu202207_1-750842714e.en.html.

The risk assessment begins with an overview of the market structure of the DeFi ecosystem and then demonstrates how threat actors misuse DeFi services to engage in and profit from illicit activity, in particular ransomware attacks, theft, fraud and scams, drug trafficking, and proliferation finance. It then considers vulnerabilities that enable the use of DeFi services for illicit purposes, including DeFi services non-compliant with AML/CFT and sanctions obligations, disintermediation, and a lack of implementation of the international AML/CFT standards in foreign countries, before highlighting mitigation measures that can address some of these vulnerabilities. The assessment includes several recommendations for the U.S. government to continue and strengthen efforts to mitigate illicit finance risks associated with DeFi services. Lastly, the assessment poses several questions that will be considered as part of the recommended actions of the assessment to address illicit finance risks.

2. Market Structure

Definition and Scope

Frequently, DeFi services purport to run without the support of a central company, group, or person, despite having a controlling organization that provides a measure of centralized administration or governance (*e.g.*, through a decentralized autonomous organization (DAO),[13] concentrated ownership or governance rights, administrative keys, or otherwise).[14] In this sense, "decentralization" claims vary in their accuracy. At times, the use of the term reflects marketing more than reality. The degree to which a purported DeFi service is in reality decentralized is a matter of facts and circumstances.

This assessment discusses services, platforms, arrangements, and products that purport to be or are commonly referred to as "decentralized" or "DeFi" in order to assess the full spectrum of risks associated with DeFi. Additionally, the assessment uses the broad term "DeFi services" to capture providers of a variety of activities, including terms broadly used by industry to include a platform, exchange, application, organization, and others. This assessment also does not evaluate the relative merits of decentralization compared to centralization. As noted above, claims of decentralization may be overstated, and the degree of decentralization of a DeFi service could change over time.

---

13 DAOs can be described as a system of administration that aspires to operate, in part, according to a set of encoded and transparent rules or smart contracts.

14 Treasury, *Action Plan to Address Illicit Financing Risks of Digital Assets*, (September 2022), https://home.treasury.gov/system/files/136/Digital-Asset-Action-Plan.pdf, p. 7.

Funds transfers between the holders of two unhosted wallets[15] that do not involve smart contracts or facilitation by a VASP[16] fall outside the scope of DeFi services for the purpose of this report.[17]

This assessment does not alter any existing legal obligations, issue any new regulatory interpretations, or establish any new supervisory expectations. The terms used in this report are intended to reflect the meanings commonly used by industry and market participants, with modifications and clarifications as appropriate. All definitions discussed in this assessment apply only within the scope of the assessment itself. They are intended only to facilitate an understanding of DeFi services and the attendant illicit finance risks.

DeFi Services and AML/CFT Regulatory Obligations

AML/CFT obligations in the United States are based on the activities in which a person engages. The BSA and its implementing regulations state that "financial institutions," such as banks, broker-dealers, mutual funds, money services businesses (MSBs), futures commission merchants (FCMs), and introducing brokers, have AML/CFT obligations.[18] These AML/CFT obligations include requirements to establish and implement an effective anti-money laundering program (AML Program)[19] and recordkeeping and reporting requirements, including suspicious activity reporting (SAR) requirements.[20]

---

15 Many virtual assets can be self-custodied and transferred without the involvement of an intermediary financial institution. The use of wallets not hosted by any financial institution or other virtual asset service provider (VASP) is commonly known as an "unhosted" or "self-hosted" wallet. Users of unhosted wallets can retain custody and transfer their virtual assets without the involvement of a financial institution.

16 As defined by FATF, virtual asset service provider, often called VASP for short, means any natural or legal person who is not covered elsewhere under the FATF Recommendations, and as a business conducts one or more of the following activities or operations for or on behalf of another natural or legal person: (i.) exchange between virtual assets and fiat currencies; (ii.) exchange between one or more forms of virtual assets; (iii.) transfer of virtual assets; (iv.) safekeeping and/or administration of virtual assets or instruments enabling control over virtual assets; and (v.) participation in and provision of financial services related to an issuer's offer and/or sale of a virtual asset. VASPs in the United States qualify as money services businesses (MSBs), and some businesses that provide virtual asset services may be required to register with federal functional regulators, depending on the services that they are providing.

17 Direct P2P transfers do not include transfers involving P2P service providers, typically natural persons engaged in the business of buying and selling virtual assets rather than safekeeping virtual assets or engaging in P2P transfers on their own behalf. P2P service providers may have regulatory requirements depending on their precise business model; Treasury, *Action Plan to Address Illicit Financing Risks of Digital Assets*, (September 2022), https://home.treasury.gov/system/files/136/Digital-Asset-Action-Plan.pdf, p. 6.

18 31 U.S.C. § 5312(a)(2); 31 C.F.R. § 1010.100(t).

19 *See* 31 C.F.R. § 1020.210 (banks); 31 C.F.R. § 1021.210 (casinos and card clubs); 31 C.F.R. § 1022.210 (MSBs); 31 C.F.R. § 1023.210 (brokers or dealers in securities); 31 C.F.R. § 1024.210 (mutual funds); 31 C.F.R. § 1026.210 (futures commission merchants and introducing brokers in commodities). An AML Program must include, at a minimum, (a) policies, procedures, and internal controls reasonably designed to achieve compliance with the provisions of the BSA and its implementing regulations; (b) independent testing for compliance; (c) designation of an individual or individuals responsible for implementing and monitoring the operations and internal controls; and (d) ongoing training for appropriate persons. Rules for some financial institutions refer to additional elements of an AML Program, such as appropriate risk-based procedures for conducting ongoing customer due diligence.

20 *See* 31 C.F.R. § 1020.320 (banks); 31 C.F.R. § 1021.320 (casinos and card clubs); 31 C.F.R. § 1022.320 (MSBs), 31 C.F.R. § 1023.320 (brokers or dealers in securities), 31 C.F.R. § 1024.320 (mutual funds), and 31 C.F.R. § 1026.320 (futures commission merchants and introducing brokers in commodities). A suspicious transaction must be reported if it is conducted or attempted by, at, or through the financial institution and the amount involved exceeds a certain threshold.

The nature of the activities in which a person engages is the key factor in determining whether and how that person must register with the Commodities Future Trading Commission (CFTC) (for FCMs and introducing brokers), the Financial Crimes Enforcement Network (FinCEN) (for MSBs), or the Securities and Exchange Commission (SEC) (for broker-dealers and mutual funds). While the degree to which a person is centralized could impact the service it provides, persons engaging in the activities of financial institutions as defined by the BSA, regardless of whether they are centralized or decentralized, will have these obligations. For example, if a DeFi service does business wholly or in substantial part in the United States and accepts and transmits virtual assets from one person to another person or location by any means, then it most likely would qualify as a money transmitter and have the same AML/CFT obligations as a money transmitter offering services in fiat currency.[21] The degree to which a service is decentralized has no bearing on these obligations so long as the service meets this definition.

Industry claims there is insufficient regulatory clarity in this space. Industry often states that there is a lack of clarity on what qualifies as a security, with which regulators they must register, and whether their DeFi services meet the definition of a financial institution under the BSA or other regulatory frameworks. Industry has also publicly engaged Treasury for additional clarity on when the deployment of software becomes covered activity under the BSA. CFTC, FinCEN, and SEC contest the perception that there is insufficient regulatory clarity, pointing to guidance they have issued over the last 10 years[22] and, with respect to the CFTC and SEC, enforcement actions against purported DeFi services that failed to comply with regulatory obligations.[23] Through public statements, guidance, and enforcement actions, these agencies have made clear that the automation of certain functions through smart contracts or computer code does not affect the obligations of financial institutions offering covered services.[24]

Further, DeFi services that are U.S. persons, like all other U.S. persons, wherever located, are required to comply with economic sanctions programs administered and enforced by Treasury's Office of Foreign Assets Control (OFAC), while non-U.S. persons also have OFAC sanctions compliance obligations in some circumstances. Sanctions compliance obligations are the same regardless of whether a transaction is denominated in virtual assets or traditional fiat currency.[25] Additionally,

---

21 *See* 31 C.F.R. 1010.100(ff)(5)(i). When DeFi services perform money transmission, the definition of money transmitter will apply to the DeFi service, the owners/operators of the DeFi service, or both. FinCEN, *FinCEN Guidance*, (May 9, 2019), https://www.fincen.gov/sites/default/files/2019-05/FinCEN%20Guidance%20CVC%20FINAL%20508.pdf, p. 18.

22 *See*, e.g., SEC, *Strategic Hub for Innovation and Financial Technology (FinHub)*, https://www.sec.gov/finhub; SEC, Crypto Assets, https://www.investor.gov/additional-resources/spotlight/crypto-assets; FinCEN, *FinCEN Guidance*, (May 9, 2019), https://www.fincen.gov/sites/default/files/2019-05/FinCEN%20Guidance%20CVC%20FINAL%20508.pdf; SEC, *Leaders of CFTC, FinCEN, and SEC Issue Joint Statement on Activities Involving Digital Assets*, (October 11, 2019), *https://www.sec.gov/news/public-statement/cftc-fincen-secjointstatementdigitalassets*; FinCEN, *Application of FinCEN's Regulations to Persons Administering, Exchanging, or Using Virtual Currencies*, (March 18, 2013), https://www.fincen.gov/sites/default/files/shared/FIN-2013-G001.pdf.

23 SEC, *Crypto Assets and Cyber Enforcement Action*, https://www.sec.gov/spotlight/cybersecurity-enforcement-actions.

24 *See*, e.g., SEC, *SEC Issues Investigative Report Concluding DAO Tokens, a Digital Asset, Were Securities*, (July 25, 2017), https://www.sec.gov/news/press-release/2017-131.

25 OFAC, *Frequently Asked Questions: Questions on Virtual Currency: 560*, https://home.treasury.gov/policy-issues/financial-sanctions/faqs/560.

in 2021 OFAC issued "Sanctions Compliance Guidance for the Virtual Currency Industry,"[26] outlining sanctions compliance obligations, reporting requirements, and best practices. OFAC subsequently has issued several Frequently Asked Questions[27] related to sanctions compliance obligations and virtual assets.

Market Overview

Building Blocks of DeFi

In DeFi, financial products and services often use smart contracts and involve various tiers of technologies that interact with one another. For the purpose of this report, DeFi technology is presented in four "layers":

The settlement tier – blockchains, including both Layer 1[28] and Layer 2[29] solutions, where the consensus state of the blockchain is maintained, i.e., where transactions are recorded, and participants and smart contracts have addresses that can hold virtual assets and interact with other participants and smart contracts.

The asset tier – virtual assets (coins and tokens) utilized in a DeFi service, including native tokens.

The protocol tier – code deployed to and executed on a blockchain, including smart contracts; this may also include auxiliary software.

The application tier – front-end user interfaces, application programming interfaces (APIs), and other code that allow participants to interact with the smart contracts and are primarily hosted off-chain.[30]

Market Participants and How They Operate

DeFi services often provide customers with the same services and products as traditional financial institutions, such as lending, borrowing, purchasing, or trading virtual assets, including assets that function as financial products like securities, commodities, derivatives, or others (*e.g.,* insurance). However, services specific to the virtual asset ecosystem, such as mixers (which functionally obfuscate the source, destination, or amount involved in a virtual asset transaction) and cross-chain bridges (which allow users to exchange virtual assets or information from one blockchain to another) may also purport to be decentralized.

---

26   Treasury, *Sanctions Compliance Guidance for the Virtual Currency Industry*, (October 2021), https://home.treasury.gov/system/files/126/virtual_currency_guidance_brochure.pdf.

27   *See* e.g., OFAC, *Frequently Asked Questions:560*, (March 19, 2018), https://home.treasury.gov/policy-issues/financial-sanctions/faqs/560; OFAC, *Frequently Asked Questions: 646*, (October 15, 2021), https://home.treasury.gov/policy-issues/financial-sanctions/faqs/5646; OFAC, *Frequently Asked Questions: 1021*, (March 11, 2022), https://home.treasury.gov/policy-issues/financial-sanctions/faqs/1021.

28   Layer 1 refers to the settlement-layer blockchain.

29   Layer 2 solutions are software on networks running on top of the settlement-layer blockchain and designed to be interoperable with the underlying Layer 1 blockchain. These Layer 2 solutions allow for transactions to occur on a separate network and eventually be recorded on the applicable blockchain. For example, Layer 2 solutions that operate with Ethereum are often marketed as cheaper and faster than Layer 1 transactions. IOSCO, *IOSCO Decentralized Finance Report*, (March 2022), https://www.iosco.org/library/pubdocs/pdf/IOSCOPD699.pdf, footnote 7.

30   IOSCO, *IOSCO Decentralized Finance Report*, (March 2022), https://www.iosco.org/library/pubdocs/pdf/IOSCOPD699.pdf.

There are likely thousands of entities offering DeFi services, although only a small number experience significant user activity[31] or have registered with regulators. One frequently cited data aggregator reportedly tracks over 2,000 DeFi services worldwide with a combined reported "total value locked" (TVL)[32] of $39.77 billion as of December 19, 2022.[33] The most prominent category of DeFi services is services that facilitate the trading of virtual assets, often called decentralized exchanges[34] (DEXs). There are reportedly 649 separate DEXs with a combined $15.85 billion in reported TVL operating as of December 19, 2022.[35] Following DEXs, lending and borrowing DeFi services reportedly have the greatest TVL at $10.85 billion across 197 separate services; there are also reportedly 60 protocols that pay users a reward for staking[36] virtual assets on the service—so-called "yield protocols"—with over $8.66 billion in reported TVL.[37] The remaining services include cross-chain bridges, liquid staking, and algorithmic stablecoins, among others, most of which are explained in the table below.

While these statistics indicate that DeFi services are an important part of the virtual asset ecosystem, they account for only a relatively small portion of total activity in virtual asset markets. According to a separate data aggregator, the 24-hour volume of total virtual asset activity in early January 2023 was $29.7 billion, with DEXs accounting for only 3 percent of the volume.[38]

---

31 Treasury, *Crypto-Assets: Implications for Consumers, Investors, and Businesses*, (September 2022), https://home.treasury.gov/system/files/136/CryptoAsset_EO5.pdf, *p. 11*.

32 TVL, an industry reported metric, is the amount of user funds deposited or "locked" in a DeFi service and is used as a measure to gauge the size of the DeFi market or the degree of adoption or acceptance by users. TVL information is not audited or verified, may double-count funds, and therefore may not be a reliable metric. *See* IMF, *Global Financial Stability Report: COVID-19, Crypto, and Climate* (2021), https://www.imf.org/en/Publications/GFSR/Issues/2021/10/12/global-financial-stability-report-october-2021.

33 Defi Llama, *TVL Rankings*, https://defillama.com.

34 The use of the term "exchange" in this assessment does not indicate registration as such or any legal status of any such platform. This definition is for the purpose of the risk assessment and should not be interpreted as a regulatory definition under the BSA or other relevant regulatory regimes.

35 Defi Llama, *TVL Rankings*, https://defillama.com.

36 Staking virtual assets refers to putting up virtual assets as collateral in a proof of stake blockchain consensus mechanism. Staked virtual assets can be destroyed as a penalty for adding invalid transactions to the blockchain, but users who stake virtual assets receive rewards for validating transactions to the blockchain.

37 *Id.*

38 CoinGecko, *Top Decentralized Exchanges Ranked by 24H Trading Volume*, accessed on January 10, https://www.coingecko.com/en/exchanges/decentralized.

Select types of DeFi services and the services they offer are illustrated in the graphic below.

Table 1

Service	Service Providers Examples	Description
Trading	DEXs	Facilitate the exchange of virtual assets through an order book exchange or liquidity pools; take deposits into liquidity pools and pay out accrued interest or other fees.[39]
Lending and Borrowing	Lending and Borrowing DeFi Services	Allow holders of virtual assets to earn a fixed or variable return on assets by depositing them in a pool that simultaneously allows other participants to borrow those assets for other financial activity.[40]
		Relatedly, some services provide "staking as a service" in which the service accepts and stakes virtual assets to participate in a proof-of-stake consensus mechanism. Some services provide "liquid staking," in which the service accepts and stakes virtual assets for users and typically issues a "liquid staking derivative" virtual asset in exchange for the staked virtual asset. Users earn a portion of staking rewards or transaction fees.
Access Across Blockchains	Cross-Chain Bridges	Facilitate network interoperability by allowing users to exchange virtual assets or information from one blockchain to another.
Mixing	Decentralized Mixers	Functionally obfuscate the source, destination, or amount involved in a virtual asset transaction. These types of services may involve centralized or decentralized mechanisms and may be effectuated using several techniques.[41]
Aggregation	Aggregators	Query a range of DeFi services to collate the best terms for a trade or other activity for users, often viewable in a single user interface; some aggregators can route transactions to fulfill desired parameters.[42]
Provision of Off-Chain Information	Oracles	Connect a smart contract to "off-chain" data, such as stock prices or off-chain collateral value, that may be an input for that smart contract's functionality.[43]
Purportedly Stable Virtual Assets	Algorithmic Stablecoin Protocols	Purport to maintain a stable value via protocols that provide for the increase or decrease of the supply of the stablecoin in response to changes in demand.[44]

---

39   IOSCO, *IOSCO Decentralized Finance Report*, (March 2022), https://www.iosco.org/library/pubdocs/pdf/IOSCOPD699.pdf, p. 14.

40   *Id.*

41   FinCEN, *Ransomware Trends in Bank Secrecy Act Data Between January 2021 and June 2021*, (October 2021), https://www.fincen.gov/sites/default/files/2021-10/Financial%20Trend%20Analysis_Ransomeware%20508%20FINAL.pdf, p. 13.

42   IOSCO, *IOSCO Decentralized Finance Report*, (March 2022), https://www.iosco.org/library/pubdocs/pdf/IOSCOPD699.pdf, pp. 15-16.

43   *Id.*, pp. 8, 33.

44   Financial Stability Board, *Regulation, Supervision, and Oversight of 'Global Stablecoin' Arrangements*, (October 13, 2020); Available at https://www.fsb.org/wp-content/uploads/P131020-3.pdf.

In DeFi services, the activities defined above are often enabled by liquidity pools, whereby users pool and lock their assets in the service's smart contract,[45] from which the DeFi service can source virtual assets for trading, lending, borrowing, and other financial services.

In the case of a DEX, liquidity pools are funded by participants who may be incentivized by a portion of fees collected by the DEX. Liquidity providers may receive a separate virtual asset from the service in exchange for locking in their assets, often referred to as a "liquidity provider token" (LP token) that entitles them to their portion of the pool, including any accrued fees.[46] Other users, accessing the liquidity pool through the DEX, can then exchange a certain quantity of one virtual asset for a certain quantity of another virtual asset. For these types of DEXs, the exchange rate between tokens is typically set by an algorithm.[47] Users often pay a fee to use the service, which is shared with LP token holders. Similarly, with liquid staking, users stake virtual assets with a DeFi service and receive a separate virtual asset in return, which represents the staked virtual assets and any accrued fees from the staking service validating transactions on the blockchain. Since LP tokens and virtual assets representing staked assets can be exchanged between different persons, it is possible for a different person than the user who original staked the asset to redeem the LP or other tokens for the assets that were initially locked in the liquidity pool.

Users may choose to trade assets via a DeFi service rather than a centralized exchange for several reasons. DEXs may purport to offer some efficiencies, such as convenient access to other DeFi services, access to a wide variety of virtual assets, or arbitrage opportunities, although in some instances they may only be able to do so because of non-compliance with applicable laws and regulations, including U.S. AML/CFT obligations and sanctions regulations. For example, when using a DEX, users are often not required to provide personal information, as typically required by many centralized exchanges that have AML/CFT and sanctions compliance programs in place. Other DeFi service users say they value the transparency of DeFi services operating on public blockchains, citing the ability to view and confirm transactions and, in many cases, view the source code of DeFi services.

Elements of Centralization

Although many services claim to be "fully decentralized," in practice there is a wide range of activity that exists on the spectrum between fully "centralized" and fully "decentralized" services. Where a service falls on this spectrum may be affected by, among other things, the governance structure of the DeFi service, access points to the service, and the settlement layer upon which the service is built. Additionally, DeFi services may seek to become more decentralized over the course of their development; for example, DeFi services often start as centralized projects with the intent of becoming more decentralized over time, and the reverse evolution is also possible.

---

45 As discussed in the custody section below in section 2.5, when users lock up assets in smart contracts, they hand over management of those assets to the smart contract and the smart contract code dictates how the asset can be transacted.

46 IOSCO, *IOSCO Decentralized Finance Report*, (March 2022), https://www.iosco.org/library/pubdocs/pdf/IOSCOPD699.pdf, p. 14.

47 Carapella, Dumas, Gerszten, Wwem, and Wall, *Decentralized Finance (DeFi): Transformative Potential & Associated Risks*, Federal Reserve Bank of Boston, Working Paper, SRA 22-02, (September 8, 2022), https://www.federalreserve.gov/econres/feds/files/2022057pap.pdf, p. 12.

In line with previous U.S. government reports, this risk assessment finds that DeFi services are in many cases decentralized more in name than in fact. Still, for DeFi services developed with opaque organizational structures, it can be more challenging to identify natural or legal persons responsible for the DeFi service.

Governance

Many DeFi services claim not to rely on a formal centralized governance structure, and organizers of DeFi services often claim to operate autonomously. In practice, however, many DeFi services continue to feature governance structures (*e.g.*, management functions, fixing problems with the code, or altering the functionality of the smart contracts to some degree).

In some cases, an owner or an operator of the DeFi service retains an administrative key, which may enable the holder to alter or disable a DeFi service's smart contracts, depending on how

> "In practice, however, many DeFi services continue to feature governance structures (*e.g.*, management functions, fixing problems with the code, or altering the functionality of the smart contracts to some degree)."

the contracts are written. In other cases, governance purports to be managed by a DAO, which can be described as a system of administration that aims to operate, in part, according to a set of encoded and transparent rules or smart contracts. DAO participants often claim that there is no central authority in a DAO and that governance is distributed across the participants. A DAO's governance token[48]—and DeFi governance (or voting) tokens in general—purport to allow disparate participants to introduce and vote on proposals determining the function of a blockchain or protocols. Governance tokens typically are tradeable on DEXs or centralized exchanges in exchange for fiat currency or other digital assets.

Governance token holders' powers and authorities vary across DeFi services. For example, in some cases, governance token holders may be permitted to vote to alter a DeFi service's smart contract, while in others, votes are more limited, such as only having the ability to vote on the process by which token holders can propose or vote on decisions or the amount of fees accrued by LP token holders. The process by which governance token holders can introduce and vote on decisions may also vary. For certain DeFi services, all governance token holders may be permitted to vote on a proposal, but only token holders that hold a specified percentage of tokens can submit proposals for a vote. The percentage of votes that constitutes passage of a decision, and the manner in which a decision is implemented, also vary by DeFi service. In some cases, decisions voted upon and approved are enacted automatically by smart contracts, while in others, owners or operators with administrative keys implement the decisions.

---

48   IOSCO, IOSCO Decentralized Finance Report, March 2022, https://www.iosco.org/library/pubdocs/pdf/IOSCOPD699.pdf, p. 24.

Moreover, distribution and concentration of governance tokens and voting demonstrate control over decentralized applications. In some services, governance tokens or voting rights may be concentrated and held by a limited number of actors. Developers and early investors in a DeFi service may keep control of the service by allocating significant shares of governance tokens to themselves or otherwise maintaining de facto control.[49] Concentration of influence within a DeFi service can also result from a low level of participation by governance token holders in voting, providing outsized voting power to the minority of token holders that do participate. Separately, some services allow for the delegation of voting rights associated with governance tokens to other persons, called delegates, while the token holder retains the economic benefits of the token.[50] In some cases, delegates accumulate significant voting rights associated with a large number of governance tokens, and this model can result in a relatively small number of delegates holding a large portion of voting power for a DeFi service.[51] Within this framework, the use of governance tokens does not necessarily equate to decentralization in decision making for the services, and the ownership of voting rights for many governance tokens can be highly concentrated.[52] As a result, in many cases a small number of persons may be able to exercise a high degree of control even if the governance structure purports to be decentralized.

The case of The DAO, a venture capital fund deployed in April 2016, demonstrates how the use of a DAO and perceived distribution of voting power does not necessarily correlate with decentralized decision making and may be subject to regulatory obligations despite a claim of decentralization.[53] In this example, the core group who deployed The DAO chose "Curators," who reviewed proposals prior to a vote, had ultimate discretion as to whether or not to submit a proposal for DAO Token holders, and could make changes to the voting process. The core group also advertised that it would submit the first proposal to The DAO. In light of these and other salient facts, the SEC determined that The DAO's investors relied on the managerial and entrepreneurial efforts of the core group and the Curators to manage The DAO and put forth project proposals that could generate profits for The DAO's investors. The facts and circumstances of that case supported an SEC determination that DAO tokens were securities, and that The DAO was an issuer of securities and required to register the offer and sale of DAO tokens.

---

49 See, e.g., Danny Nelson & Tracy Wang, Master of Anons: How a Crypto Developer Faked a DeFi Ecosystem, Coindesk (August 4, 2022), https:// www.coindesk.com/layer2/2022/08/04/master-of-anons-how-a-crypto-developer-faked-a-defi-ecosystem. For further discussion of governance in decentralized finance, see Sirio Aramonte, Wenqian Huang & Andreas Schrimpf, supra note 29, at 27-29. See also Igor Makarov & Antoinette Schoar, Cryptocurrencies and Decentralized Finance (DeFi), The Brookings Institution, (2022), https://www.brookings.edu/wpcontent/uploads/2022/03/SP22_BPEA_MakarovSchoar_conf-draf.pdf.

50 IOSCO, IOSCO Decentralized Finance Report, (March 2022), https://www.iosco.org/library/pubdocs/pdf/IOSCOPD699.pdf, p. 41.

51 Id.

52 One recent analysis found that among several major DAOs, less than 1% of token holders controlled 90% of the voting power. See Chainalysis, Dissecting the DAO: Web3 Ownership is Surprisingly Concentrated, (June 27, 2022), https://blog.chainalysis.com/reports/web3-daos-2022. Also, the amount of governance tokens a user must either own or be delegated to raise new proposals may be extremely high.

53 SEC, Report of Investigation Pursuant to Section 21(a) of the Securities Exchange Act of 1934:The DAO, (July 25, 2017), https://www.sec.gov/litigation/investreport/34-81207.pdf.

The CFTC enforcement actions against bZeroX, LLC, its founders, and its successor entity Ooki DAO allege that individuals who participate in DAO governance processes may be deemed to be members of an unincorporated association who can potentially be held personally liable for the association's debts. As set forth in greater detail below, the CFTC in September 2022 issued an order simultaneously filing and settling charges against bZeroX, LLC and its two founders for various violations of the Commodity Exchange Act (CEA) and related CFTC Regulations and, at the same time, filed a federal court lawsuit against the Ooki DAO alleging the same violations. As part of that case, among other things, the CFTC's order found that the Ooki DAO was an unincorporated association of which the two founding members were actively participating members and thus personally liable for the Ooki DAO's violations.[54] Similarly, in a federal court action, in upholding the CFTC's service on the Ooki DAO, the U.S. District Court for the Northern District of California held that the Ooki DAO had the capacity to be sued as an unincorporated association under applicable law.[55]

Application Layer

While users of DeFi services can conduct activities by engaging directly with the smart contracts on a blockchain, users usually rely on applications or websites that make interacting with DeFi services more user-friendly and can include analytics that can be used to inform transactions. In most instances, application developers are critical to DeFi services' usability. Application developers can have meaningful effects on the degree to which users are able to use a DeFi service effectively, even if they purport not to exercise "control" over the DeFi service's smart contracts or are not necessarily token holders who play a role in its governance structure. As one example, Polymarket, an online trading platform offering event-based binary options,[56] deployed smart contracts to support operation of its markets.[57] While users could transact directly with the smart contracts, in order to do so they needed to interface with Polymarket's website, as the underlier to every Polymarket binary option—whether a political event or the future price of Bitcoin—was only specifically identifiable through the Polymarket website. As this case indicates, information provided via applications can thus be integral to transactions using DeFi infrastructure.

---

54 CFTC, CFTC Imposes $250,000 Penalty Against bZeroX, LLC and Its Founders and Charges Successor Ooki DAO for Offering Illegal, Off-Exchange Digital-Asset Trading, Registration Violations, and Failing to Comply with Bank Secrecy Act, (September 22, 2022), https://www.cftc.gov/PressRoom/PressReleases/8590-22.

55 CFTC v. Ooki DAO, No. 3:22-cv-05416-WHO, 2022 WL 17822445, at *5-12 (N.D. Cal. December 20, 2022).

56 According to the order, through its website, Polymarket offered the public the opportunity to "bet on your beliefs" by buying and selling binary options contracts related to an event taking place in the future that are susceptible to a "yes" or "no" resolution, such as: "Will $ETH (Ethereum) be above $2,500 on July 22?"; "Will the 7-day average COVID-19 case count in the U.S. be less than 15,000 for the day of July 22"; "Will Trump win the 2020 presidential election?". See CFTC, CFTC Orders Event-Based Binary Options Markets Operator to Pay $1.4 Million Penalty, (January 3, 2022), https://www.cftc.gov/PressRoom/PressReleases/8478-22.

57 CFTC, Order Instituting Proceedings Pursuant To Section 6(C) And (D) Of The Commodity Exchange Act, Making Findings, And Imposing Remedial Sanctions, (January 3, 2022), https://www.cftc.gov/media/6891/enfblockratizeorder010322/download; see section 4.1 of this report for additional information on the CFTC's order filing and settled charges against Polymarket.

Settlement Layer

Blockchains can also vary in degrees of decentralization. Most blockchains on which DeFi services operate are permissionless, meaning that users require no prior approval to participate in network activities.[58] However, some blockchains have a limited number of participants in their consensus mechanism, often referred to as validators, to confirm the transactions that have taken place and post them to the blockchain. While a blockchain with a small number of validators can enable faster settlement time to the blockchain and potentially lower fees, it can also concentrate decision making for approving transactions. This could enable a small group of persons to make decisions about the types of transactions that are supported by the blockchain, including the ability to approve certain transactions, or the order in which transactions are settled. For example, persons with sufficient mining power or staked virtual assets[59] could prioritize their own transactions over others'. Even blockchains with hundreds of thousands of validators can experience concentration if a small group of persons commands a large portion of mining power, staked virtual assets, proposed transaction blocks, or other means of controlling the consensus mechanism.

Custody

Some DeFi services purport to allow users to self-custody their virtual assets through their own digital wallets, claiming that users retain control over their virtual assets during interactions with the DeFi service. The retention of the virtual asset by a user will depend, however, on the type of DeFi service with which the participant is engaging. In many DeFi services, users are required to deposit or lock their virtual assets in a smart contract. In some cases, an individual, group of individuals, or entity will retain an administrative key, as noted above, to that smart contract or otherwise be able to change the smart contract and, as such, may have effective control over participant assets.[60] For example, in the case of bZx DAO/Ooki DAO described above, the DAO was able to access and control the operation of, and funds held in, the relevant bZx Protocol smart contracts.[61] The use of the administration keys was determined by votes of DAO token holders.

---

58 President's Working Group on Financial Markets, the Federal Deposit Insurance Corporation, and the Office of the Comptroller of the Currency, Report on Stablecoins, (November 2021), https://home.treasury.gov/system/files/136/ StableCoinReport_Nov1_508.pdf, p. 13.

59 Mining power refers to the ability of validators in a proof of work model to complete mathematical computations, which requires expensive computer equipment and energy, to record and validate transactions to the blockchain. Generally, the larger amount of mining power or staked virtual assets a validator has, the more often they will be responsible for approving transactions to the blockchain and accruing transaction fees.

60 IOSCO, *IOSCO Decentralized Finance Report*, (March 2022), https://www.iosco.org/library/pubdocs/pdf/IOSCOPD699. pdf, pp. 22-23.

61 Complaint at ¶ 41.d, CFTC v. Ooki DAO, No. 3:22-cv-05416, ECF #1, (N.D. Cal. September 22, 2022).

3. Illicit Finance Threats

Illicit actors, including cyber criminals and fraudsters, abuse DeFi services to launder illicit proceeds. They also take advantage of cybersecurity weaknesses, compromising DeFi services to steal virtual assets. In particular, the DPRK, under pressure from U.S., European, and United Nations (UN) sanctions regime, increasingly steals virtual assets from both centralized VASPs and DeFi services. DPRK and other actors' abuse of DeFi services is explored in more detail below. This assessment does not specifically address the possible role of DeFi services in terrorist financing.

This risk assessment draws extensively on case examples Treasury identified and analyzed in its research. However, final adjudication and public discussion of cases often takes years to complete. Given how recently the DeFi market has developed and expanded, there were relatively few case examples that this assessment could include. The number of case studies does not, however, reflect the level of risk identified in this assessment. The risk assessment was also informed by consultations with several U.S. government Departments and Agencies and the over 75 responses to Treasury's September 2022 Request for Comment, which was issued in conjunction with the publication of the Action Plan (see Annex A on methodology).

Money Laundering

There have been several instances of actors, including ransomware actors, thieves, scammers, and drug traffickers, using DeFi services to transfer and launder their illicit proceeds. These actors use a variety of techniques and services to accomplish this, including exchanging virtual assets for other virtual assets that are easier to use in the virtual asset industry or less traceable, sometimes using cross-chain bridges to exchange virtual assets for others that operate on other blockchains; sending virtual assets through mixers; and placing virtual assets in liquidity pools as a form of layering. Steps that criminals take involving DeFi services may not be for the specific purpose of obfuscation but could instead be to move illicit proceeds generated from thefts from DeFi services. For the purpose of this report, this is considered in the section on money laundering, as it is part of an overall process to enable criminals to profit from their crimes. While the objective of the money laundering process by malign actors using DeFi services remains the same, criminals may use new means to do so, for example through chain hopping.

In many cases, criminals use DeFi services for these purposes without being required to provide customer identification information. This can make DeFi services more appealing to criminals than centralized VASPs, which are more likely to implement AML/CFT measures.

These laundering methods can create challenges for investigators attempting to trace illicit proceeds, and many actors will use more than one of the techniques below. The level of sophistication will likely depend on the individual actor's technical experience and familiarity with virtual assets and DeFi services. However, law enforcement has observed even lesser-skilled actors using some of the techniques below.

- **DEXs and Cross-Chain Bridges**: Often, illicit actors will use DeFi services, such as a DEX, to convert one virtual asset into a different virtual asset. As described above, this could be done for a variety of reasons, including to exchange into a more liquid asset that has higher trading volumes and is easier to cash out into fiat currency. This is similar to how illicit actors may exchange stolen funds in a lesser-used fiat currency for U.S. dollars, which are more widely accepted, or into another currency that allows them to evade U.S. sanctions. Criminals may also use DEXs to exchange virtual assets into another virtual asset that is compatible with a cross-chain bridge, mixer, or other DeFi service; to exchange one virtual asset for another with weaker illicit finance mitigation or less centralized control; or to exchange for an asset that is less traceable. Actors may choose to exchange their illicit proceeds for several different assets, sometimes using different DEXs to obtain better conversion rates and diversify their laundering methods. Illicit actors can also chain-hop, exchanging virtual assets on one blockchain for virtual assets on another, which could be done through a DEX or aggregator or by interacting directly with a cross-chain bridge. Chain-hopping can make it more difficult for competent authorities to trace financial transactions or for service providers to detect if incoming funds are tied to illicit activity. This is especially true if actors are using specific assets or blockchains that are more difficult to trace given current limits on blockchain analysis.

- **Mixers**: Criminals also use virtual asset mixers to functionally obfuscate the source, destination, or amount involved in a transaction. Mixers can accomplish this through a variety of mechanisms, including: pooling or aggregating virtual assets from multiple individuals, wallets, or accounts into a single transaction or transactions; splitting an amount into multiple amounts and transmitting the virtual assets as a series of smaller independent transactions; or leveraging code to coordinate, manage, or manipulate the structure of the transaction; among other methods.[62] Mixing services may be advertised as a way to evade AML/CFT requirements and rarely, if ever, include the capacity and willingness to provide upon request to regulators or law enforcement the resulting transactional chain or information collected as part of the transaction.[63] As such, mixers can functionally simulate a customer depositing funds from an anonymous account into a financial institution's omnibus account and withdrawing funds into a separate anonymous account.

- **Liquidity Pools:** Illicit actors can place criminals' proceeds in a DeFi service's liquidity pool, where the assets provide liquidity to support trades on the service. As noted above, liquidity providers typically lock their virtual assets into the liquidity pool and may receive a portion of fees or some other type of return or interest created through the DeFi service.[64] By placing funds into liquidity pools, actors may generate funds from trading fees.

After criminals have layered the funds or converted them to the desired virtual assets using DeFi services, they may use centralized VASPs to exchange virtual assets for fiat currency. Often, these VASPs have weak or non-existent AML/CFT controls and operate or are incorporated

---

62 These descriptions are for the purpose of this risk assessment and should not be interpreted as a regulatory description under the BSA or other relevant regulatory regimes.

63 See e.g., Treasury, U.S. Treasury Issues First-Ever Sanctions on a Virtual Currency Mixer, Targets DPRK Cyber Threats, (May 6, 2022), https://home.treasury.gov/news/press-releases/jy0768; FinCEN, First Bitcoin "Mixer" Penalized by FinCEN for Violating Anti-Money Laundering Laws, (October 19, 2020), https://www.fincen.gov/news/news-releases/first-bitcoin-mixer-penalized-fincen-violating-anti-money-laundering-laws.

64 IOSCO, *IOSCO Decentralized Finance Report*, (March 2022), https://www.iosco.org/library/pubdocs/pdf/IOSCOPD699.pdf, p. 14.

or headquartered in jurisdictions that have not effectively implemented international AML/CFT standards for virtual assets.[65] In other cases, rather than exchanging for fiat currency, launderers may let their virtual assets sit unused in liquidity pools or unhosted wallets or use the virtual assets to fund future criminal activity directly. For example, cybercriminals can in some cases use virtual assets to purchase technological tools, infrastructure, or services to enable additional attacks or exploits.

The sections below explain in detail several of the key threats for which criminals have used DeFi services to profit from their illicit activity. In many of the examples below, illicit actors use DeFi services not only to launder or exchange illicit proceeds, but also to commit underlying predicate crimes through hacks and heists of DeFi service.

Ransomware

The severity and sophistication of ransomware attacks has risen in recent years.[66] Ransomware is a national security priority and an area of significant concern to the U.S. government in terms of potential loss of life, financial effects, and critical infrastructure vulnerability.[67] A FinCEN analysis of SAR data found that reported ransomware-related incidents more than doubled in 2021 compared to 2020, with ransomware-related filings in 2021 approaching $886 million in value.[68] Ransomware actors have increasingly targeted larger enterprises to demand larger payouts, with a median ransomware-related payment amount of $135,000, based on the same analysis.[69] Ransomware actors can use DeFi services to exchange virtual assets from ransomware-related payments for other virtual assets and decentralized mixers to obfuscate the movement of funds.70 For example, one blockchain analytics firm identified that one cross-chain bridge was used to launder ransomware proceeds from over 13 ransomware strains. According to this report, ransomware actors laundered over $50 million through the cross-chain bridge in the first half of 2022. [71]

---

65   FATF, Targeted Update On Implementation Of The FATF Standards On Virtual Assets And Virtual Asset Service Providers, (June 2022), https://www.fatf-gafi.org/media/fatf/documents/recommendations/Targeted-Update-Implementation-FATF%20Standards-Virtual%20Assets-VASPs.pdf.

66   See Internet Crime Complaint Center, Annual Reports, with (1) 2021 IC3 Annual Report, (2) 2020 IC3 Annual Report, (3) 2019 IC3 Annual Report, and (4) 2018 IC3 Annual Report.

67   Treasury, *National Money Laundering Risk Assessment*, (February 2022), https://home.treasury.gov/system/files/136/2022-National-Money-Laundering-Risk-Assessment.pdf; Treasury, Treasury Continues Campaign to Combat Ransomware As Part of Whole-of-Government Effort, (Oct. 15, 2021), https://home.treasury.gov/news/press-releases/jy0410; DOJ, *U.S. Government Launches First One-Stop Ransomware Resource at StopRansomware.gov*, (Jul. 15, 2021), https://www.justice.gov/opa/pr/us-government-launches-first-one-stopransomware-resource-stopransomwaregov; FinCEN, *Advisory on Ransomware and the Use of the Financial System to Facilitate Ransom Payments*, (November 8, 2021), https://www.fincen.gov/sites/default/files/2021-11/FinCEN%20Ransomware%20Advisory_FINAL_508_.pdf.

68   FinCEN, *Financial Trend Analysis: Ransomware Trends in Bank Secrecy Act Data Between July 2021 and December 2021*, (November 2022), https://www.fincen.gov/sites/default/files/2022-11/Financial%20Trend%20Analysis_Ransomware%20FTA%202_508%20FINAL.pdf, p. 2.

69   *Id.* at p. 6.

70   FinCEN, *Ransomware Trends in Bank Secrecy Act Data Between January 2021 and June 2021*, (October 2021), https://www.fincen.gov/; FinCEN, *Ransomware Trends in Bank Secrecy Act Data Between January 2021 and June 2021*, (October 2021), https://www.fincen.gov/sites/default/files/2022-11/Financial%20Trend%20Analysis_Ransomware%20FTA%202_508%20FINAL.pdf.

71   Elliptic, *The State of Cross-Chain Crime*, (October 4, 2022), https://www.elliptic.co/resources/state-of-cross-chain-crime-report, p. 26-27.

Cybercriminals often use remote desktop protocol endpoints[72] and phishing campaigns to harvest credentials or otherwise gain access to a victim's computer network.[73] Ransomware actors have also shared resources, such as exploit kits,[74] or formed partnerships with other cybercriminals to enhance the effectiveness of their attacks. Some ransomware developers sell access to their malware to affiliates in a "ransomware-as-a-service" model, thereby decreasing the barrier to entry and level of technical expertise required to conduct ransomware attacks. In addition, ransomware actors increasingly employ double extortion tactics, where criminals steal confidential data before encrypting it and threaten to publish the data if the victim does not pay the ransom.

Theft

In 2022, illicit actors stole billions of dollars' worth of virtual assets from VASPs, including DeFi services. DeFi services have been particularly lucrative for cybercriminals, accounting for a majority of stolen virtual assets in 2022, according to one blockchain analytics company.[75] Cyber criminals are increasingly exploiting vulnerabilities in the smart contracts governing DeFi services to steal virtual assets, causing investors to lose money.[76] Cyber criminals have sought to take advantage of

> "In 2022, illicit actors stole billions of dollars' worth of virtual assets from VASPs, including DeFi services."

investors' increased interest in virtual assets, as well as the complexity of cross-chain functionality and the open source nature of DeFi services. After stealing funds, cyber criminals often use the techniques discussed above to exchange and move stolen assets to maximize profits from the theft. For example, criminals that have stolen platform-specific assets, like governance tokens of small DeFi services, may look to quickly exchange the stolen assets for more liquid virtual assets using DeFi services to avoid detection and a loss in price if other token holders also decide to sell as a result of a breach. Types of thefts in the virtual asset space include security breaches, code exploits, and flash loan attacks, described below.

- In a **security breach**, an attacker penetrates a victim's security controls to conduct unauthorized transactions, including sending funds from a victim's account to one controlled by the hacker. The victim may be an individual or the blockchain firm itself, whose credentials may be compromised through phishing, key logging, or social engineering.

---

72 Remote Desktop Protocol is a proprietary network protocol that allows an individual to control the resources and data of a computer over the Internet; Federal Bureau of Investigation (FBI), *Cyber Actors Increasingly Exploit the Remote Desktop Protocol to Conduct Malicious Activity*, (September 27, 2018), https://www.ic3.gov/Media/Y2018/PSA180927.

73 Treasury, *Action Plan to Address Illicit Financing Risks of Digital Assets*, (September 2022), https://home.treasury.gov/system/files/136/Digital-Asset-Action-Plan.pdf.

74 Exploit kits are toolkits that automate the identification and exploitation of client-side vulnerabilities.

75 TRM Labs, *DeFi, Cross-Chain Bridge Attacks Drive Record Haul from Cryptocurrency Hacks and Exploits*, (December 16, 2022), https://www.trmlabs.com/post/defi-cross-chain-bridge-attacks-drive-record-haul-from-cryptocurrency-hacks-and-exploits.

76 FBI, *Cyber Criminals Increasingly Exploit Vulnerabilities in Decentralized Finance Platforms to Obtain Cryptocurrency, Causing Investors to Lose Money*, (August 29, 2022), https://www.ic3.gov/Media/Y2022/PSA220829.

- In **code exploits**, hackers find vulnerabilities in the code of smart contracts and leverage them to remove funds from DeFi services without authorization. Hackers can also use the discovered vulnerabilities to carry out attacks against the service. The exploitation of code vulnerabilities may trigger immediate copycat hacks, such as those conducted by automated trading bots.[77]

- In a **flash loan**[78] **attack**, the attacker manipulates the logic of the underlying smart contract's code so that all technical requirements are met, and the transaction is posted to the blockchain despite the attacker paying back only a small portion (or none) of the principal loan. In some cases, the attacker uses the temporary surge of funds obtained in a flash loan to manipulate prices of virtual assets, often through the interaction of multiple DeFi services. This enables attackers to take over the governance of a smart contract or protocol, change the code, and drain the treasury in a very compressed timeframe.[79]

Case Examples

- In January 2023, the CFTC filed a civil enforcement action charging Avraham Eisenberg with a scheme to unlawfully obtain over $110 million in digital assets from Mango Markets, a purported decentralized digital asset exchange, through a price inflation scheme using "oracle manipulation."[80] The CFTC alleged that to accomplish the scheme, Eisenberg created two anonymous accounts on Mango Markets, which he used to establish large leveraged positions in a swap contract based on the relative value of MNGO, the "native" token of Mango Markets, and USDC, a stablecoin. Eisenberg then allegedly artificially pumped up the price of MNGO by rapidly purchasing substantial quantities of MNGO on three digital asset exchanges that were the inputs for the "oracle," or data feed, used to determine the value of Eisenberg's swap positions, resulting in a temporary, artificial spike in the value of Eisenberg's swap positions on Mango Markets. The CFTC alleged that Eisenberg then cashed out his illicit profits by using the artificially inflated value of his swaps as collateral to withdraw over $110 million in digital assets from Mango Markets. In a separate indictment filed in January 2023, the U.S. Attorney's Office for the Southern District of New York charged Eisenberg with commodities fraud, commodities market

---

77 *See* e.g. The Block, *Polychain-backed DFX Finance hacked for $7.5 million*, (November 11, 2022), https://www.theblock.co/post/185796/polychain-dfx-finance-hacked.

78 "Flash loans" enable users to borrow, use, and repay virtual assets in a single transaction that is recorded on the blockchain in the same data block. Because there is no default risk associated with flash loans, users can borrow without posting collateral and without risk of being liquidated; Treasury, *Crypto-Assets: Implications for Consumers, Investors, and Businesses*, (September 2022), https://home.treasury.gov/system/files/136/CryptoAsset_EO5.pdf, footnote 118.

79 *Id.*, footnote 118, ; *see also* Shaurya Malwa, *Solana DeFi Protocol Nirvana Drained of Liquidity After Flash Loan Exploit*, Coindesk (July 28, 2022), https://www.coindesk.com/tech/2022/07/28/solana-defi-protocol-nirvana-drained-of-liquidity-after-flash-loan-exploit.

80 CFTC, *CFTC Charges Avraham Eisenberg with Manipulative and Deceptive Scheme to Misappropriate Over $110 million from Mango Markets, a Digital Asset Exchange*, (January 9, 2023) https://www.cftc.gov/PressRoom/PressReleases/8647-23#:~:text=The%20complaint%20alleges%20that%20on,Mango%20Markets%2C%20which%20he%20used.

manipulation, and wire fraud.[81] Eisenberg was also charged by the SEC in connection with his alleged manipulation of the MNGO token.[82]

- In November 2022, the Department of Justice (DOJ) announced that James Zhong pled guilty to committing wire fraud in September 2012 when he unlawfully obtained over 50,000 Bitcoin from the Silk Road dark web internet marketplace. In September 2012, Zhong executed a scheme to defraud Silk Road of its money and property by (a) creating a string of approximately nine Silk Road accounts in a manner designed to conceal his identity; (b) triggering over 140 transactions in rapid succession in order to trick Silk Road's withdrawal-processing system into releasing approximately 50,000 Bitcoin from its Bitcoin-based payment system into Zhong's accounts; and (c) transferring this Bitcoin into a variety of separate addresses also under Zhong's control, all in a manner designed to prevent detection, conceal his identity and ownership, and obfuscate the Bitcoin's source.[83] As part of this process, Zhong allegedly pushed approximately 750 Bitcoin of the Silk Road crime proceeds through a decentralized Bitcoin mixer.[84] In November 2021, law enforcement seized over 50,000 Bitcoin from Zhong's home, which was then the largest cryptocurrency seizure in DOJ history and was the Department's second-largest financial seizure ever as of November 2022.[85]

Fraud and Scams

Multiple U.S. government agencies track and publish virtual asset-related complaints by the public, which have indicated a sharp increase in losses related to virtual assets.[86] Federal agencies have also issued warnings related to their findings, including noting a material increase in virtual assets as a payment method for all types of scams.[87] In fact, in 2021, the Federal Bureau of Investigation (FBI) Internet Crime Complaint Center (IC3) reported that while the number of complaints associated with virtual assets decreased by approximately 3 percent in 2021, the loss amount reported in

---

81 DOJ, *Alleged Perpetrator Of $100 Million Crypto Market Manipulation Scheme To Make Initial Appearance In The Southern District Of New York*, (February 2, 2023), https://www.justice.gov/usao-sdny/pr/alleged-perpetrator-100-million-crypto-market-manipulation-scheme-make-initial.

82 SEC, *Manipulating Mango Markets' "Governance Token" to Steal $116 Million of Crypto Assets*, (January 20, 2023), https://www.sec.gov/news/press-release/2023-13.

83 DOJ, *U.S. Attorney Announces Historic $3.36 Billion Cryptocurrency Seizure And Conviction In Connection With Silk Road Dark Web Fraud*, (November 7, 2022), https://www.justice.gov/usao-sdny/pr/us-attorney-announces-historic-336-billion-cryptocurrency-seizure-and-conviction.

84 DOJ, *Affidavit in Support of Government's Forfeiture Motion, s1 14 Cr. 68 (LGS)*, (November 7, 2022), https://www.justice.gov/usao-sdny/press-release/file/1549821/download, p. 17.

85 DOJ, *U.S. Attorney Announces Historic $3.36 Billion Cryptocurrency Seizure And Conviction In Connection With Silk Road Dark Web Fraud*, (November 7, 2022), https://www.justice.gov/usao-sdny/pr/us-attorney-announces-historic-336-billion-cryptocurrency-seizure-and-conviction.

86 Treasury, *Crypto-Assets: Implications for Consumers, Investors, and Businesses*, (September 2022), https://home.treasury.gov/system/files/136/CryptoAsset_EO5.pdf, p. 25-26; *see* summarized statistics from the FBI, Consumer Financial Protection Bureau, and the Federal Trade Commission.

87 United States Secret Service, *Combating the Illicit Use of Digital Assets*, https://www.secretservice.gov/investigation/DigitalAssets.

virtual asset-related IC3 complaints increased by nearly 600 percent, from $246 million in 2020 to more than $1.6 billion in 2021.[88] These schemes often result in significant losses for the victims.

> "The loss amount reported in virtual asset-related IC3 complaints increased by nearly 600 percent, from $246 million in 2020 to more than $1.6 billion in 2021."

These scams are committed by a variety of actors and use an assortment of techniques, including "rug pulls" and "pig butchering" schemes.

- In a "**rug pull**," a scammer raises investments funds in a seemingly legitimate project before ending the project and stealing invested funds. Rug pulls may involve scammers creating and contributing to a liquidity pool in a DeFi service in the form of a new virtual asset, often a stablecoin. One form of a rug pull is executed when, after a creator promotes the asset to investors to increase the demand and thereby increase the price of the virtual asset, the creator withdraws their contributions from the liquidity pool abruptly, causing the price of the new virtual asset to crash. Rug pulls may also involve restrictions on investors selling assets or may involve the coding of an explicit, malicious backdoor into a new virtual asset smart contract that enables the developer to pull out assets from a liquidity pool all at once.[89]

- **"Pig Butchering"** is where scammers initiate and develop relationships with victims and pressure them to invest in fake investment platforms that enable the scammer to steal invested funds.[90] These scammers encounter victims on dating apps, social media websites, or even text messages sent to appear inadvertently sent to the wrong number. After a scammer has developed trust with their target over a period of weeks or months, they will introduce the idea of making an investment using virtual assets and use confidence-building techniques to convince victims that they are investing in a legitimate virtual asset opportunity. A common iteration of the scam directs users to access fraudulent investment websites through virtual asset wallet applications where vulnerabilities are exploited to provide full access and control of victims' wallets to the scammers.

Case Examples

- In June 2022, the DOJ and law enforcement partners announced that Le Anh Tuan, 26, a Vietnamese national, was charged with one count of conspiracy to commit wire fraud and one count of conspiracy to commit international money laundering in the Central District of California in connection with a scheme involving the "Baller Ape"

---

88 FBI, *2021 Internet Crime Report*, (2021), https://www.ic3.gov/Media/PDF/AnnualReport/2021_IC3Report.pdf

89 Financial Stability Oversight Council (FSOC), *Report on Digital Asset Financial Stability Risks and Regulation*, (2022), https://home.treasury.gov/system/files/261/FSOC-Digital-Assets-Report-2022.pdf, p. 32.

90 DOJ, *Court Authorizes the Seizure of Domains Used in Furtherance of a Cryptocurrency "Pig Butchering" Scheme*, (November 21, 2022), https://www.justice.gov/usao-edva/pr/court-authorizes-seizure-domains-used-furtherance-cryptocurrency-pig-butchering-scheme; FINRA, Pig Butchering Scams: What They Are and How to Avoid Them," (December 13, 2022), https://www.finra.org/investors/insights/pig-butchering-scams.

non-fungible token (NFT).[91] Tuan allegedly was involved in the Baller Ape Club, an NFT investment project that purportedly sold NFTs in the form of various cartoon figures, often including the figure of an ape. According to the indictment, shortly after the first day Baller Ape Club NFTs were publicly sold, Tuan and his co-conspirators engaged in a "rug pull," ending the purported investment project, deleting its website, and stealing the investors' money. Based on blockchain analytics, shortly after the rug pull, Tuan and his co-conspirators allegedly laundered investors' funds through "chain-hopping," a form of money laundering in which one type of coin is converted to another type and funds are moved across multiple cryptocurrency blockchains and used decentralized cryptocurrency swap services to obscure the trail of Baller Ape Club investors' stolen funds. In total, Tuan and his co-conspirators allegedly obtained approximately $2.6 million from investors.

- In March 2022, the DOJ, Internal Revenue Service-Criminal Investigation, Department of Homeland Security, and the U.S. Postal Inspection Service announced that Ethan Nguyen and Andre Llacuna were charged in a criminal complaint with conspiracy to commit wire fraud and conspiracy to commit money laundering, in connection with an alleged million-dollar scheme to defraud purchasers of NFTs advertised as "Frosties." Rather than providing the benefits advertised to Frosties NFT purchasers, Nguyen and Llacuna allegedly transferred the cryptocurrency proceeds of the scheme to various cryptocurrency wallets under their control.[92] As alleged in the criminal complaint, after the Frosties NFT sale was publicly denounced as a fraud on social media, substantial amounts of Ether (ETH) were sent from wallets associated with the defendants to Tornado Cash smart contracts. Those smart contracts later transferred ETH to a wallet address that ultimately deposited the funds into wallets owned by the defendants.

Drug Trafficking

Drug trafficking organizations are growing more comfortable with darknet markets[93] and the use of virtual assets generally to launder funds, including increased use of DeFi services, according to law enforcement assessments and analysis by blockchain analytic firms. For example, one blockchain analytics company identified that drug-focused darknet markets generated nearly $2 billion in virtual assets in 2021 through sales, representing a steady increase in revenue since 2018.[94] Still, the size and scope of drug proceeds generated on the darknet and laundered via virtual assets remain low in comparison to cash-based retail street sales.[95] In addition to darknet market sales

---

91 DOJ, *Justice Department Announces Enforcement Action Charging Six Individuals with Cryptocurrency Fraud Offenses in Cases Involving Over $100 Million in Intended Losses*, (June 30, 2022), https://www.justice.gov/usao-cdca/pr/justice-department-announces-enforcement-action-charging-six-individuals-cryptocurrency.

92 DOJ, *Two Defendants Charged In Non-Fungible Token ("NFT") Fraud And Money Laundering Scheme*, (March 24, 2022), https://www.justice.gov/usao-sdny/pr/two-defendants-charged-non-fungible-token-nft-fraud-and-money-laundering-scheme-0; https://www.justice.gov/usao-sdny/press-release/file/1486846/download.

93 DOJ, *International Law Enforcement Operation Targeting Opioid Traffickers on the Darknet Results in 150 Arrests Worldwide and the Seizure of Weapons, Drugs, and over $31 Million*, (October 26, 2021), https://www.justice.gov/opa/pr/international-lawenforcement-operation-targeting-opioid-trafickers-darknet-results-p. 150.

94 Chainalysis, *The 2022 Crypto Crime Report*, p. 100.

95 DOJ, *International Law Enforcement Operation Targeting Opioid Traffickers on the Darknet Results in 150 Arrests Worldwide and the Seizure of Weapons, Drugs, and over $31 Million*, (October 26, 2021), https://www.justice.gov/opa/pr/international-lawenforcement-operation-targeting-opioid-trafickers-darknet-results-p. 150.

in drugs, law enforcement assesses that certain drug traffickers are increasingly converting fiat currency proceeds into virtual assets for laundering.[96]

Proliferation Finance

Under pressure from robust U.S. and UN sanctions, the DPRK has resorted to illicit activities, including cyber-enabled heists from VASPs and other financial institutions, to generate revenue for its unlawful weapons of mass destruction (WMD) and ballistic missile programs.[97] The U.S.

> "On March 23, 2022, the Lazarus Group, a U.S.-sanctioned, DPRK state-sponsored cyber hacking group, carried out the largest virtual assets heist to date, worth almost $620 million, from a blockchain project linked to the online game Axie Infinity."

government has observed DPRK cyber actors targeting organizations in the virtual asset industry, including DeFi services (see text box below).[98] For example, on March 23, 2022, the Lazarus Group, a U.S.-sanctioned, DPRK state-sponsored cyber hacking group, carried out the largest virtual assets heist to date, worth almost $620 million, from a blockchain project linked to the online game Axie Infinity.[99] The group also stole $100 million worth of virtual assets from a cross-chain bridge called Horizon.[100] In addition to heists, DPRK-linked actors are involved in other illicit activity related to virtual assets, including ransomware attacks[101] and the use of virtual asset applications modified to include malware to facilitate the theft of virtual assets.[102] DPRK has also dispatched thousands of highly skilled internet technology (IT) workers around the world who often take on projects involving virtual assets. These IT workers earn revenue for the DPRK that contributes to its weapons programs, and the privileged access these workers gain as contractors can enable DPRK's malicious cyber intrusions or support DPRK money laundering activities.[103] The U.S. government has observed DPRK actors using the techniques described above to launder the illicit proceeds from these activities.

---

96   United Nations Office on Drugs and Crime, *World Drug Report 2021: Global Overview: Drug Demand Drug Supply*, (June 2021), https://www.unodc.org/res/wdr2021/field/WDR21_Booklet_2.pdf, p. 76.

97   Treasury, *U.S. Treasury Issues First-Ever Sanctions on a Virtual Currency Mixer, Targets DPRK Cyber Threats*, (May 6, 2022), https://home.treasury.gov/news/press-releases/jy0768.

98   CISA, *TraderTraitor: North Korean State-Sponsored APT Targets Blockchain Companies*, (April 18, 2022), https://www.cisa.gov/uscert/ncas/alerts/aa22-108a.

99   FBI, *FBI Statement on Attribution of Malicious Cyber Activity Posed by the Democratic People's Republic of Korea*, (April 14, 2022), https://www.fbi.gov/news/press-releases/fbi-statement-on-attribution-of-malicious-cyber-activity-posed-by-the-democratic-peoples-republic-of-korea; Treasury, *Treasury Designates DPRK Weapons Representatives*, (November 8, 2022), https://home.treasury.gov/news/press-releases/jy1087.

100 Treasury, *U.S. Treasury Issues First-Ever Sanctions on a Virtual Currency Mixer*, Targets DPRK Cyber Threats, (May 6, 2022), https://home.treasury.gov/news/press-releases/jy0768; FBI, *FBI Confirms Lazarus Group Cyber Actors Responsible for Harmony's Horizon Bridge Currency Theft*, (January 23, 2023), https://www.fbi.gov/news/press-releases/fbi-confirms-lazarus-group-cyber-actors-responsible-for-harmonys-horizon-bridge-currency-theft.

101 Cybersecurity and Infrastructure Security Agency (CISA), *North Korean State-Sponsored Cyber Actors Use Maui Ransomware to Target the Healthcare and Public Health Sector*, (July 6, 2022), https://www.cisa.gov/uscert/ncas/alerts/aa22-187a.

102 CISA, *AppleJeus: Analysis of North Korea's Cryptocurrency Malware*, (February 17, 2021), https://www.cisa.gov/uscert/ncas/alerts/aa21-048a.

103 Department of State, Treasury, and FBI, *Guidance on the Democratic People's Republic of Korea Information Technology Workers*, (May 16, 2022), https://home.treasury.gov/system/files/126/20220516_dprk_it_worker_advisory.pdf.

> **TraderTraitor: North Korean State-Sponsored Advanced Persistent Threat (APT) Targets Blockchain Companies, Including DeFi Protocols**
>
> The FBI, the Cybersecurity and Infrastructure Security Agency (CISA), and Treasury issued a joint Cybersecurity Advisory (CSA) to highlight the cyber threat associated with virtual asset thefts and tactics used by a DPRK state-sponsored APT group[104] since at least 2020.[105] The U.S. government has observed DPRK cyber actors targeting a variety of organizations in the blockchain technology and virtual asset industry, including virtual asset exchanges, DeFi protocols, play-to-earn virtual asset video games, cryptocurrency trading companies, venture capital funds investing in virtual assets, and individual holders of large amounts of virtual assets or valuable NFTs. The activity described in the advisory involves social engineering of victims using a variety of communication platforms to encourage individuals to download trojanized virtual asset applications on Windows or Mac operating systems. The cyber actors then use the applications to gain access to the victim's computer, propagate malware across the victim's network environment, and steal private keys or exploit other security gaps. These activities enable additional follow-on activities that initiate fraudulent blockchain transactions.

Case Example

In November 2022, OFAC redesignated Tornado Cash under E.O. 13722 and E.O. 13694, as amended, for its role in enabling malicious cyber activities that ultimately support the DPRK's WMD program. Tornado Cash, an entity that provides virtual asset mixing services, obfuscated the movement of over $455 million worth of virtual assets stolen in March 2022 by the OFAC-designated, DPRK-controlled Lazarus Group, in the largest known virtual currency heist to date. Malicious cyber actors subsequently used the Tornado Cash smart contracts to launder more than $96 million of funds derived from the June 24, 2022 Harmony Bridge Heist and at least $7.8 million from the August 2, 2022 Nomad Heist.[106]

In connection with the November 2022 action, OFAC stated that sanctions were applied to the entity known as Tornado Cash and that Tornado Cash uses computer code known as "smart contracts" to implement its governance structure, provide mixing services, offer financial incentives for users, increase its user base, and facilitate the financial gain of its users and developers. OFAC also explained that Tornado Cash's organizational structure consists of: (1) its founders and other associated developers, who together launched the Tornado Cash mixing service, developed new Tornado Cash mixing service features, created the Tornado Cash DAO, and actively promoted the platform's popularity in an attempt to increase its user base; and (2) the Tornado Cash DAO, which is responsible for voting on and implementing new features created by the developers.[107]

---

104 This group is commonly tracked by the cybersecurity industry as Lazarus Group, APT38, BlueNoroff, and Stardust Chollima.

105 CISA, *TraderTraitor: North Korean State-Sponsored APT Targets Blockchain Companies*, (April 18, 2022), https://www.cisa.gov/uscert/ncas/alerts/aa22-108a.

106 Treasury, *Treasury Designates DPRK Weapons Representatives*, (November 8, 2022), https://home.treasury.gov/news/press-releases/jy1087.

107 OFAC, *Frequently Asked Questions: 1095*, (November 8, 2022), https://home.treasury.gov/policy-issues/financial-sanctions/faqs/added/2022-11-08.

4. Vulnerabilities

Non-Compliant DeFi Services in the United States

DeFi services at present often do not implement AML/CFT controls or other processes to identify customers, allowing layering of proceeds to take place instantaneously and pseudonymously, using long strings of alphanumeric characters rather than names or other personally identifying information. DeFi services engaged in activity covered by the BSA have AML/CFT obligations, and all DeFi services subject to U.S. jurisdiction have sanctions compliance obligations, regardless of their status as covered financial institutions. When these entities fail to register with the appropriate regulator, fail to establish and maintain sufficient AML/CFT controls, or do not comply with sanctions obligations, criminals are more likely to exploit their services successfully, including to circumvent U.S. and UN sanctions.

> "DeFi services at present often do not implement AML/CFT controls or other processes to identify customers, allowing layering of proceeds to take place instantaneously and pseudonymously."

Despite these requirements, several DeFi projects have affirmatively touted alack of AML/CFT controls as one of the primary goals of decentralization. For instance, one VASP announced in 2021 that it would transition from a traditional corporate structure into a DAO for the purpose of ceasing to collect customer information for AML/CFT compliance, although in practice this would not have impacted the service's BSA obligations.[108] Similarly, founders of an unregistered FCM argued that transitioning to a DAO would insulate the FCM from U.S regulatory oversight and accountability for compliance with U.S. law. These examples indicate that the lack of compliance may be due in part to gaps in common views between industry and regulators of how relevant laws and regulations, including securities, commodities, and money transmission regulations, apply to DeFi services. The assessment recognizes that the public nature of the blockchain and the role of centralized VASPs in accessing fiat currency can partially mitigate this and other vulnerabilities. They are explored further with other mitigation measures in sections 5.2 and 5.3, respectively.

Regulators have pursued cases against DeFi services operating in the United States that failed to register with the appropriate regulators and failed to implement the requisite AML/CFT program for the services they provide.

Case Example

- As discussed above, the CFTC in September 2022 issued an order simultaneously filing and settling charges against a company, bZeroX LLC, and its two founders for illegally

---

108 *See* Gary Silverman, *Cryptocurrency: Rise of Decentralized Finance Sparks 'Dirty Money' Fears*, Financial Times (September 15, 2021), https://www.ft.com/content/beeb2f8c-99ec-494b-aa76-a7be0bf9dac6; William Foxley, *ShapeShift Is Going Full DeFi to Lose KYC Rules*, Coindesk (January 6, 2021), https://www.coindesk.com/business/2021/01/06/shapeshift-is-going-full-defi-to-lose-kyc-rules/; DOJ, *The Report of the Attorney General Pursuant to Section 5(b)(iii) of Executive Order 14067: The Role Of Law Enforcement In Detecting, Investigating, And Prosecuting Criminal Activity Related To Digital Assets*, (September 2022), https://www.justice.gov/d9/2022-12/The%20Report%20of%20the%20Attorney%20General%20Pursuant%20to%20Section.pdf, p. 10.

offering leveraged and margined retail commodity transactions in digital assets; engaging in activities only registered FCMs can lawfully perform; and failing to adopt a customer identification program as part of a BSA compliance program, as required of FCMs.[109] Simultaneously, the CFTC filed a federal civil enforcement action in the U.S. District Court for the Northern District of California charging a DAO—the successor to the original company that operated the same software protocol—with violating the same laws as the original company and founder. Neither the original company nor the DAO maintained a required customer identification program, and the lack of AML measures was explicitly advertised as a positive feature of the service.

As part of the case, the CFTC's order found that bZeroX transferred control of the Protocol to the bZx DAO, which is now doing business as the Ooki DAO. By transferring control to a DAO, bZeroX's founders touted to bZeroX community members the operations would be enforcement-proof, allowing the Ooki DAO to violate the CEA and CFTC regulations with impunity, as alleged in the federal court action. The CFTC order found the DAO was an unincorporated association of which the two founding members were actively participating members and liable for the Ooki DAO's violations of the CEA and CFTC regulations. Similarly, in the federal court action, in upholding the CFTC's service on the Ooki DAO, the U.S. District Court for the Northern District of California held that the Ooki DAO had the capacity to be sued as an unincorporated association under applicable law.[110]

- The CFTC in January 2022 entered an order filing and simultaneously settling charges against a Delaware-registered company for offering off-exchange event-based binary options contracts and failure to obtain designation as a designated contract market or registration as a swap execution facility.[111] The company created, defined, and resolved the contracts for the event-based binary option markets offered through its website and recorded on the blockchain. Market participants could open accounts only with an email address and a username and fund their "Polymarket Wallets" for trading with an Ethereum-based "stablecoin" cryptocurrency pegged to the value of the U.S. dollar. To operate its markets, the company deployed smart contracts, which are programmable self-executing contracts hosted on a blockchain. While users could transact directly with the smart contracts, in order to understand the definition of the event market contract with which they are transacting, they needed to interface with Polymarket's website, which was owned and operated by the Delaware corporation with its headquarters in New York and made available to U.S. customers.

- In August 2021, the SEC charged two individuals and their Cayman Islands-based company for unregistered sales of more than $30 million in securities using smart

---

109 CFTC, *CFTC Imposes $250,000 Penalty Against bZeroX, LLC and Its Founders and Charges Successor Ooki DAO for Offering Illegal, Off-Exchange Digital-Asset Trading, Registration Violations, and Failing to Comply with Bank Secrecy Act*, (September 22, 2022), https://www.cftc.gov/PressRoom/PressReleases/8590-22.

110 *CFTC v. Ooki DAO*, No. 3:22-cv-05416-WHO, 2022 WL 17822445, at *5-12 (N.D. Cal. Dec. 20, 2022).

111 CFTC, *CFTC Orders Event-Based Binary Options Markets Operator to Pay $1.4 Million Penalty*, (January 3, 2022), https://www.cftc.gov/PressRoom/PressReleases/8478-22.

contracts and so-called DeFi technology and for misleading investors concerning the operations and profitability of their business "DeFi Money Market."[112] The SEC's order found that the respondents used smart contracts to sell two types of digital tokens: one that could be purchased using specified digital assets and that paid a given percent interest, and another so-called "governance token" that purportedly gave holders certain voting rights, a share of excess profits, and the ability to profit from token resales in the secondary market. The order found that the two types of tokens were offered and sold as securities and that respondents had violated the registration and antifraud provisions of the federal securities laws. The order also found that the respondents misrepresented how the company was operating, violating the SEC's anti-fraud provisions, and publicly touted that they required no "Know Your Customer" documentation. Without admitting or denying the findings in the order, the respondents consented to a cease-and-desist order, including disgorgement totaling more than $12 million and penalties of $125,000 for each of the individual respondents.

In some cases, the lack of a clear organizational structure may make it difficult to identify any person, group of persons, or entity operating a DeFi service, whether because no such person exists or because of distributed, poor, or purposefully confusing organization. This poses critical challenges for conducting supervision and, when appropriate, enforcement against DeFi services that are not fulfilling their AML/CFT obligations.[113] This challenge can be compounded by the fast pace of change in the virtual asset industry, the large and growing number of DeFi services, and limited resources at some regulatory agencies.[114]

Disintermediation

Many virtual assets can be self-custodied and transferred without the involvement of an intermediary financial institution, which can be referred to as disintermediation. For example, users of unhosted wallets can retain custody of and transfer their virtual assets without the involvement of a regulated financial institution. Many DeFi services claim to be disintermediated by enabling automated P2P transactions without the need for an account or custodial relationship. Whether an entity operating in the DeFi space is a covered financial institution under the BSA depends on specific facts and circumstances surrounding its financial activities. To the extent a DeFi service falls outside the current definition of a financial institution under the BSA, a vulnerability may exist due to the reduced likelihood that such DeFi services would choose to implement AML/CFT measures like assessing illicit finance risks, establishing an AML program, or reporting suspicious

---

112 SEC, *SEC Charges Decentralized Finance Lender and Top Executives for Raising $30 Million Through Fraudulent Offerings*, (August 6, 2021), https://www.sec.gov/news/press-release/2021-145.

113 DOJ, *The Report of the Attorney General Pursuant to Section 5(b)(iii) of Executive Order 14067: The Role Of Law Enforcement In Detecting, Investigating, And Prosecuting Criminal Activity Related To Digital Assets*, (September 2022), https://www.justice.gov/d9/2022-12/The%20Report%20of%20the%20Attorney%20General%20Pursuant%20to%20Section.pdf, p. 10.

114 Treasury, *National Strategy for Combating Terrorist and Other Illicit Financing*, (May 2022), https://home.treasury.gov/system/files/136/2022-National-Strategy-for-Combating-Terrorist-and-Other-Illicit-Financing.pdf, p. 14 ("Significant resource constraints at FinCEN, the IRS, and state and territorial financial regulators have materially affected their ability to effectively supervise and examine certain non-bank financial institutions, which may include those posing higher risk").

activity. In cases in which a DeFi service falls outside of the scope of the BSA, this can result in gaps in suspicious activity reporting and limit authorities' collection of and access to information critical to supporting financial investigations. A DeFi service's claim that it is or plans to be "fully decentralized" does not impact its status as a financial institution under the BSA.

Cross-Border Nature and Gaps in AML/CFT Regimes across Countries

The 2022 NRAs identified that the most significant illicit financing risk associated with virtual assets stemmed from VASPs operating abroad with substantially deficient AML/CFT programs, particularly in jurisdictions where AML/CFT standards for virtual assets are nonexistent or not effectively implemented. This remains a key vulnerability with DeFi services, as DeFi services may fall under the VASP definition established by the FATF.

Uneven and often inadequate regulation and supervision internationally allows illicit actors to engage in regulatory arbitrage, which is compounded by the nearly instantaneous and borderless nature of virtual asset transfers. This potentially exposes the U.S. financial system to VASPs, including some DeFi services, with deficient or nonexistent AML/CFT controls operating abroad. VASPs may choose to operate in jurisdictions with minimal or nonexistent AML/CFT requirements, weak supervision of their legal frameworks, or both. Of 53 jurisdictions that FATF assessed as of June 2022, four years after the FATF amended the standards to apply to virtual assets and VASPs, the majority still require significant improvements on implementing these standards.[115] Of the assessed jurisdictions, 33 have received partially compliant ratings, and 8 have received non-compliant ratings. Additionally, less than half of jurisdictions that responded to a FATF-administered voluntary survey in March 2022 had introduced a licensing or registration regime for virtual assets and VASPs.

Given that many countries are still in the early stages of developing AML/CFT regimes for virtual assets and VASPs, few jurisdictions likely have assessed the risks associated with DeFi services, considered how they could fit into their regulatory regime, and allocated supervisory and enforcement resources for the virtual asset sector. In particular, jurisdictions have highlighted that they face challenges attempting to identify which DeFi entities should be regulated and how to consistently enforce national obligations that implement the FATF standards for such entities.[116]

Additionally, some VASPs claim not to have a headquarters or jurisdiction in which they are subject to regulatory obligations, including AML/CFT requirements. This is the case with several DeFi services that purport to have distributed governance models. Other VASPs have adopted a distributed organizational architecture under which they register in one country, have personnel in a second country, and offer services in several countries with different legal and regulatory approaches to virtual assets. For example, some countries' AML/CFT regimes apply if a DeFi service offers services to customers or operates within their jurisdiction. In other places, the key factor that triggers licensing or registration is whether the jurisdiction is the primary location

---

115 FATF, *Targeted Update On Implementation Of The FATF Standards On Virtual Assets And Virtual Asset Service Providers*, (June 2022), https://www.fatf-gafi.org/media/fatf/documents/recommendations/Targeted-Update-Implementation-FATF%20Standards-Virtual%20Assets-VASPs.pdf.

116 *Id.*, p. 20.

in which business is performed, where business books or records physically reside, or otherwise. Differences and gaps in these approaches can complicate regulation, supervision, and enforcement, which often require considerable cooperation amongst authorities.

Cyber-Related Vulnerabilities

DeFi services are often particularly vulnerable to large-scale thefts due to a combination of factors, including aggregation of large amounts of funds, the lack of requirements for cybersecurity and audits in the DeFi space, concentrated administrator rights, and the availability of open-source code for DeFi services' smart contracts. As noted above, these vulnerabilities can be exploited by hackers through security breaches, code exploits, and flash loan attacks. The documented efforts of nation-state cyber groups or other illicit actors to steal or fraudulently acquire money, including

> "The documented efforts of nation-state cyber groups or other illicit actors to steal or fraudulently acquire money, including virtual assets, present a national security concern."

virtual assets, present a national security concern. The noted cybersecurity gaps of DeFi services leave their operations vulnerable to theft and fraud, which also present risks for consumers and the virtual asset industry.

- Cross-chain bridges in particular can be attractive targets for hackers because they often feature a central storage point of funds that back the bridged assets on the receiving blockchain.[117] Regardless of how those funds are stored—locked up in a smart contract or with a centralized custodian—that storage point can become a target. For similar reasons, the treasuries and liquidity pools of DeFi services are also common targets.

- Secure code development is a difficult undertaking even in the best of circumstances, and large software firms may struggle to deploy secure products. Conversely, DeFi services are usually small enterprises that operate in a market without binding or normative requirements for cybersecurity. While some services perform code audits, there is a lack of standardization in audits, and several DeFi services have been exploited even after claiming successful audits. To educate users and DeFi service developers about these vulnerabilities, in August 2022 the FBI published a public service announcement recommending that users research DeFi services; ensure that the services have conducted audits; and be aware of risks posed by crowdsourced solutions to vulnerability identification and patching.[118] The announcement encouraged DeFi services to institute real-time analytics, monitoring, and rigorous testing of code to identify and respond to

---

117 Chainalysis, *Vulnerabilities in Cross-chain Bridge Protocols Emerge as Top Security* Risk, (August 2, 2022), https://blog. chainalysis.com/reports/cross-chain-bridge-hacks-2022/; TRM Labs, DeFi, *Cross-Chain Bridge Attacks Drive Record Haul from Cryptocurrency Hacks and Exploits*, (December 16, 2022), https://www.trmlabs.com/post/defi-cross-chain-bridge-attacks-drive-record-haul-from-cryptocurrency-hacks-and-exploits.

118 FBI, *Cyber Criminals Increasingly Exploit Vulnerabilities in Decentralized Finance Platforms to Obtain Cryptocurrency, Causing Investors to Lose Money*, (August 29, 2022), https://www.ic3.gov/Media/Y2022/PSA220829.

vulnerabilities and to develop and implement, when appropriate, an incident response plan. Per the text box above, the U.S. government issued a Cybersecurity Advisory in April 2022 about the DPRK targeting virtual asset firms, which provided information on tactics, techniques, and procedures and indicators of compromise to stakeholders in the virtual asset industry to identify and mitigate cyber threats.[119]

- As discussed above, the administration of a DeFi service's infrastructure may be more concentrated than advertised, enabling the targeting of an individual or small group with administrator rights to compromise the entire network.[120]

- Many DeFi services purport to make their code viewable to the public, which can increase transparency and users' confidence in the services and enable viewers to identify opportunities for code improvement. This can also, however, provide opportunities for cybercriminals to review the code and identify potential exploits to enable theft or other misuses.[121] This vulnerability can be compounded if the smart contracts are not written carefully or if they lack a mechanism for quick deactivation or alternations if a critical exploit is identified. As such, it is critical that the DeFi service identify and address vulnerabilities and potential exploits in open-source code. Depending on the particular factual circumstances, however, such code exploits may not always map neatly onto the elements of the criminal statutes used most often in fraud or computer intrusion cases, especially in instances where the code itself allows for the exploitation to take place.[122]

The public availability of many DeFi services' source code also presents the opportunity for other persons to reuse the code in smart contracts for a separate DeFi service. This could lead to widespread exploits if code reused in multiple DeFi services contains vulnerabilities. It also means that persons can "fork" the smart contracts, creating a clone of a DeFi services' source code, potentially with some modifications. As such, even if a DeFi service or related persons were subject to enforcement or law enforcement actions and required to cease operations, another person could simply "copy and paste" the code to re-constitute the DeFi service. Additionally, the original DeFi service source code could continue running and be available for use unless there is a person willing and able to deactivate it. The utility of the source code and re-constituted services, however, could be limited by a lack of liquidity or users.

5. Mitigation Measures

The U.S. government's assessments of risk take into consideration the effect of mitigating measures, including regulation, supervision, and enforcement. The below section explains regulatory frameworks at the global and domestic levels for DeFi services. It also explores the mitigating effects of elements specific to the virtual asset and DeFi ecosystem, including the transparency of public blockchains, the role of centralized VASPs to access fiat currency, and potential industry

---

119 CISA, *TraderTraitor: North Korean State-Sponsored APT Targets Blockchain Companies*, (April 18, 2022), https://www.cisa.gov/uscert/ncas/alerts/aa22-108a.

120 To gain access to four out of the five validating nodes necessary to take control of the Ronin Bridge network and steal $620 million worth of cryptocurrency, DPRK-associated persons sent a PDF file containing malware to a single engineer; Cnet.com, *A Fake Job Offer Reportedly Led to Axie Infinity's $600 Million Hack*, (July 6, 2022), https://www.cnet.com/personal-finance/crypto/a-fake-job-offer-reportedly-led-to-axie-infinitys-600m-hack/.

121 DOJ, *The Report of the Attorney General Pursuant to Section 5(b)(iii) of Executive Order 14067: The Role Of Law Enforcement In Detecting, Investigating, And Prosecuting Criminal Activity Related To Digital Assets*, (September 2022), https://www.justice.gov/d9/2022-12/The%20Report%20of%20the%20Attorney%20General%20Pursuant%20to%20Section.pdf, p. 10.

122 *Id.*

solutions. The assessment finds that these measures may partially mitigate illicit finance risks but do not sufficiently address the identified vulnerabilities.

Regulatory Frameworks

The AML/CFT regulatory framework in the United States, discussed above in section 2.2, is a foundational mitigation measure to address illicit finance risks associated with DeFi services that are operating in the United States. Additionally, work in international forums, in particular the FATF, can also play an important role in developing standards and promoting implementation of those standards to address illicit finance risks associated with DeFi services.

FATF

In 2018, the FATF revised its standards to apply similar rules for virtual assets and VASPs as those in existence for other kinds of financial services providers.

In 2019 and again in 2021 the FATF further elaborated on these standards in guidance. In its 2021 Updated Guidance for a Risk-based Approach for Virtual Assets and VASPs ("Updated Guidance"), FATF examined how virtual assets activities and VASPs, including some DeFi services, fall within the scope of the FATF Standards. With regards to DeFi services, the FATF clarified that the software programs themselves are not VASPs under the FATF Standards, meaning that the standards do not apply to underlying software or technology. However, the Updated Guidance highlighted that DeFi services often have a central party with some measure of involvement or control, such as creating and launching a virtual asset, developing service functions and user interfaces for accounts holding an administrative "key," or collecting fees. In such cases, DeFi services may fall under the FATF definition of a VASP and therefore have AML/CFT obligations. In particular, the Updated Guidance emphasizes that, since DeFi services are often not decentralized in practice, marketing terms or self-identification as a DeFi service or the specific technology involved do not determine if its owner or operator is a VASP. Still, under the FATF standards, DeFi services that lack an entity with sufficient control or influence over the service may not be explicitly subject to AML/CFT obligations under the FATF standards,[123] which could lead to potential gaps for DeFi services in other jurisdictions.

Public Blockchain Transparency

As noted above, transactions involving DeFi services often occur on the public blockchain, which means that any person with access to the internet can view the pseudonymous transaction data in a public ledger for the blockchain. Because most DeFi services also conduct transactions using smart contracts that are settled on the blockchain rather than through an internal order book or ledger, the pseudonymous transaction information is viewable and traceable on a blockchain's public ledger.

Public ledgers can support investigations by competent authorities in tracing the movement of illicit proceeds. While the ledgers do not contain names or traditional account identifiers associated

---

123 The FATF standards that apply to all individuals (like targeted financial sanctions) would still apply to DeFi services, regardless of structure.

with any particular address, regulators and law enforcement can in some cases take viewable pseudonymous user and transaction information and pair it with other pieces of information to identify transaction participants. The transparency of blockchains can complicate attempts to move or obfuscate funds even pseudonymously.[124] For instance, a wallet address publicly identified with a hack may be the subject of intense public scrutiny, making it hard to launder proceeds in that wallet, even though its owner remains unknown. Financial institutions, regulatory agencies, and law enforcement may use multiple complementary third-party tools to identify, trace, and attribute virtual asset transactions on most virtual asset blockchains.[125] Currently, these tools support hundreds of virtual assets and use clustering algorithms, web scraping, scam database monitoring, and other methods to enable an investigator to link and attribute a wide range of transactions to real-world individuals and entities.[126] The tools can generate transaction graphs, which allow users to visualize and present complex associations. Records from the blockchain have been admitted as evidence in court cases, and blockchain analysis was determined to be a reliable foundation for probable cause for a search warrant application.[127] Blockchain analytics can also be a useful tool for the private sector to provide information on risk, support a risk-based approach to compliance, and review customer activity at onboarding and on a periodic or event-triggered basis.[128]

However, there are some limitations to relying on public blockchain information and tracing to mitigate illicit finance risks in the DeFi space. First, as noted above, the data on the public blockchain is pseudonymous. While regulators, law enforcement, and public blockchain companies can in some cases identify transaction participants, they may in other cases only have the participants' wallet addresses without additional identifying information. Additionally, users can obfuscate the tracing of transactions on the public blockchain through the use of mixers, cross-chain bridges, or anonymity-enhanced cryptocurrencies (AECs), which can create challenges for blockchain tracing. Second, blockchain tracing and analytics often require an initial identified illicit transaction or address as a starting point, although new tools are able to identify potentially suspicious activity based on blockchain data. Third, critical activities in a DeFi service can occur off-chain and there are challenges to locating and obtaining this data.

Moreover, several virtual asset industry participants are exploring measures to increase privacy for virtual asset transactions, including the use of Layer 2 technology, or private blockchains, for which public ledgers will not be viewable and blockchain tracing will not be applicable. While the

---

124 Treasury, *Action Plan to Address Illicit Financing Risks of Digital Assets*, (September 2022), https://home.treasury.gov/system/files/136/Digital-Asset-Action-Plan.pdf, p. 6.

125 DOJ, *The Report of the Attorney General Pursuant to Section 5(b)(iii) of Executive Order 14067: The Role Of Law Enforcement In Detecting, Investigating, And Prosecuting Criminal Activity Related To Digital Assets*, (September 2022), https://www.justice.gov/d9/2022-12/The%20Report%20of%20the%20Attorney%20General%20Pursuant%20to%20Section.pdf, p. 32

126 *Id.*

127 *In the Matter of the Search of Multiple Email Accounts Pursuant to 18 U.S.C. § 2703 for Investigation of Violation of 18 U.S.C. § 1956 et al.*, Case No. 20-sc-3310 (D.D.C.), (August 26, 2021), https://www.dcd.uscourts.gov/sites/dcd/files/20sc3310-Opinion.pdf.

128 FinCEN, *Prepared Remarks of Alessio Evangelista, Associate Director, Enforcement and Compliance Division, During Chainalysis Links Conference*, (May 19, 2022), https://www.fincen.gov/news/speeches/prepared-remarks-alessio-evangelista-associate-director-enforcement-and-compliance; Treasury, *Sanctions Compliance Guidance for the Virtual Currency Industry*, (October 2021), https://home.treasury.gov/system/files/126/virtual_currency_guidance_brochure.pdf, p. 16.

U.S. government supports privacy enhancing technologies that simultaneously allow for or even promote compliance with AML/CFT obligations, the use of non-public blockchains by entities that do not comply with AML/CFT obligations or services that may fall outside current regulations will heighten AML/CFT risks.

Finally, licenses to use blockchain for tracing are expensive and require extensive training, and as noted above, these blockchain tracing tools use methods for analyzing transaction data that may not apply to all blockchains or virtual assets, meaning the industry has a lack of visibility into transactions involving those blockchains or virtual assets.[129]

Use of Centralized VASPs as On- and Off-Ramps

While DeFi users may need to access centralized VASPs to exchange virtual assets for fiat currency to buy goods and services, reliance on AML/CFT programs of centralized VASPs only partially mitigates the risks associated with non-compliant DeFi services. Many centralized VASPs are themselves non-compliant with international AML/CFT standards and often based in jurisdictions with weak or non-existent AML/CFT requirements. Additionally, there are identified cases of centralized VASPs that are subject to the requirements of the BSA yet fail to implement the requisite AML programs for the services they provide.[130] Moreover, even a centralized VASP with a strong AML program may face challenges in tracing virtual assets when users have leveraged DeFi services to obfuscate the source of funds.

While centralized VASPs are currently needed as on- and off-ramps for many transactions, further adoption of virtual assets may reduce this necessity in the future. At present, most merchants and businesses and many financial institutions do not accept virtual assets as a means of payment, and consumers often cannot use virtual assets to pay for goods and services. As such, virtual asset users often need to exchange virtual assets for fiat currency to buy goods and services, and DeFi service users frequently require centralized VASPs to access fiat currency. Still, the ability to use virtual assets to pay for goods and services is increasing.[131] While some merchants may use third-party services that have AML/CFT obligations, the growing use of virtual assets as payment for goods and services could decrease the role of centralized VASPs.

The U.S. government will continue efforts to improve implementation of international AML/CFT standards abroad and compliance by VASPs with AML/CFT and sanctions obligations in

---

129   DOJ, *The Report of the Attorney General Pursuant to Section 5(b)(iii) of Executive Order 14067: The Role Of Law Enforcement In Detecting, Investigating, And Prosecuting Criminal Activity Related To Digital Assets*, (September 2022), https://www.justice.gov/d9/2022-12/The%20Report%20of%20the%20Attorney%20General%20Pursuant%20to%20Section.pdf, pp. 43-44.

130   *See* e.g., Treasury, *Settlement Agreement between the U.S. Department of the Treasury's Office of Foreign Assets Control and Payward, Inc. ("Kraken")*, https://home.treasury.gov/policy-issues/financial-sanctions/recent-actions/20221128; (November 28, 2022), Treasury, *Treasury Announces Two Enforcement Actions for over $24M and $29M Against Virtual Currency Exchange Bittrex, Inc.*, (October 11, 2022), https://home.treasury.gov/news/press-releases/jy1006; FinCEN, *First Bitcoin "Mixer" Penalized by FinCEN for Violating Anti-Money Laundering Laws*, (October 19, 2020), https://www.fincen.gov/news/news-releases/first-bitcoin-mixer-penalized-fincen-violating-anti-money-laundering-laws.

131   Bitpay and PYMNTS.com, *Paying with Cryptocurrency: What Consumers and Merchants Expect from Digital Currencies*, (June 2022), https://www.pymnts.com/wp-content/uploads/2022/06/PYMNTS-Paying-With-Cryptocurrency-June-2022.pdf; Deloitte, *Merchants Getting Ready for Crypto: Merchant Adoption of Digital Currency Payments Survey*, (2022), https://www2.deloitte.com/content/dam/Deloitte/us/Documents/technology/us-cons-merchant-getting-ready-for-crypto.pdf.

the United States and abroad. However, the present reliance on centralized VASPs to comply with AML/CFT and sanctions obligations is not likely to sufficiently mitigate illicit finance risks associated with DeFi services.

Potential Industry Solutions

Several entities in the virtual asset industry are developing AML/CFT and sanctions compliance solutions for DeFi services or other tools that could be used to mitigate illicit finance risks associated with DeFi. Technological innovation of this kind could potentially bolster the accessibility, transparency, and security of the U.S. financial system, but most tools remain too nascent for definitive conclusions on their promise. Many potential solutions are designed to support various elements of compliance with AML/CFT obligations while maximizing user privacy, including through digital identity technology to support identity verification by DeFi services that can be informed by a user's transaction history on the public blockchain. Zero-knowledge proofs[132] can also enable a DeFi service user to confirm that their identity has been verified without revealing personal information. Industry solutions may also enable illicit finance risk mitigations to be integrated into smart contract code, such as restricting transaction frequency; placing threshold limits for certain customer types; or using oracles[133] to screen against virtual asset wallet addresses appearing on sanctions lists and to prevent sanctioned addresses from using a DeFi service. While some of these solutions may be applicable to the broader virtual asset ecosystem and financial system, DeFi services may provide an interesting use case given the use of smart contracts and the wealth of data available via the public blockchain. Such solutions could support compliance with BSA and sanctions obligations for obliged DeFi services but could also be used voluntarily by DeFi services not subject to AML/CFT obligations to mitigate risks.

It is important to note, however, that criminals likely will seek to take advantage of gaps in potential solutions, and many tools require further technical development and adjustments to meet AML/CFT requirements. As such, it will be critical for relevant virtual asset entities to consider and address potential illicit finance risks before launch. Private sector firms and developers have raised questions—some of which are still to be addressed—about how to effectively meet AML/CFT and sanctions compliance obligations, and public-private sector engagement will play a critical role in the development of these solutions. Treasury is working to improve the overall effectiveness of the AML/CFT regulatory framework and sanctions compliance programs in the virtual asset space and will engage with the private sector to support responsible innovation in the DeFi space.

---

132 A cryptographic scheme where a prover is able to convince a verifier that a statement is true, without providing any more information than that single bit (that is, that the statement is true rather than false); National Institute of Standards and Technology, *Glossary: Zero-Knowledge Proof*, https://csrc.nist.gov/glossary/term/zero_knowledge_proof.

133 *See* Table 1 for definition of "oracle."

6. Conclusion, Recommended Actions, and Posed Questions

This risk assessment finds that criminals use DeFi services to profit from illicit activity, in particular ransomware, theft, scams, drug trafficking, and proliferation finance.

Key factors, such as non-compliant DeFi services, disintermediation, a lack of implementation of the international AML/CFT standards in foreign countries, and cybersecurity weaknesses in DeFi services, continue to pose vulnerabilities that enable criminal use of DeFi services to profit from illicit activity. While existing regulatory frameworks, transparency afforded by the public blockchain, the role of centralized VASPs in the virtual asset ecosystem, and industry solutions can partially mitigate some of these vulnerabilities, the identified vulnerabilities still pose residual illicit finance risks associated with DeFi services. This report recognizes, however, that illicit activity is a subset of overall activity within the DeFi space and, at present, the DeFi space remains a minor portion of the overall virtual asset ecosystem. Moreover, money laundering, proliferation financing, and terrorist financing most commonly occur using fiat currency or other traditional assets as opposed to virtual assets.

Treasury has identified the following areas for further work to address these risks.

Recommended Actions

- **Strengthen U.S. AML/CFT Supervision of Virtual Asset Activities:** The U.S. government should work to strengthen existing supervisory and enforcement functions to increase and harmonize compliance with AML/CFT and other regulatory requirements, including for DeFi services with BSA obligations. As part of this effort, regulators should conduct additional outreach to industry to further explain how applicable regulations apply to DeFi services, in line with previously issued regulations and guidance. Based on feedback from industry, regulators should also consider taking additional regulatory actions and issuing additional guidance to provide further clarity.

- **Assess Possible Enhancements to the U.S. AML/CFT Regulatory Regime as Applied to DeFi Services:** Treasury will continue to evaluate the U.S. AML/CFT requirements to ensure that the U.S. framework effectively safeguards the U.S. financial system from all manner of threats and illicit financial activity, whether facilitated by fiat currency or virtual assets. The assessment recommends enhancing the U.S. AML/CFT regime as applied to DeFi services by closing any identified gaps in the BSA to the extent that they allow certain DeFi services to fall outside the scope of the BSA's definition of financial institutions.

- **Continue Research, Private Sector Engagement to Support Understanding of Developments in DeFi Ecosystem:** DeFi services have the potential to become more or less decentralized over the course of their evolution; for example, they often start out as centralized projects with decentralization as an end goal. The U.S. government should continue to monitor any changes in the DeFi ecosystem that could affect illicit finance risks or the application of AML/CFT obligations to entities in the space. The U.S. government should do this through research and engagement with the private sector.

- **Continue to Engage with Foreign Partners:** The U.S. government will continue working with foreign partners bilaterally and through multilateral fora to close gaps in implementation of the international standards with regards to virtual assets and VASPs. This will include sharing the findings of this report and encouraging partners to assess illicit finance risks associated with DeFi services and to develop and implement mitigation measures. Additionally, the United States at the FATF will press for immediate implementation of the FATF standards and advocate for FATF members to continue to monitor developments in DeFi and facilitate dialogue and mutual support on common AML/CFT implementation challenges, risk assessments, and good practices.

- **Advocate for Cyber Resilience in Virtual Asset Firms, Testing of Code, and Robust Threat Information Sharing**: The United States should continue to advocate for DeFi services to institute real time analytics, monitoring, and rigorous testing of code in order to more quickly identify vulnerabilities and respond to indicators of suspicious activity. The U.S. government should continue to, as available and appropriate, share information with virtual asset firms and the public about potential threats and mitigation measures that firms can take to improve defenses.

- **Promote Responsible Innovation of Mitigation Measures:** Several entities in the virtual asset industry are developing AML/CFT solutions for DeFi services or other tools that could be used by the virtual asset industry to mitigate illicit finance risks associated with DeFi. The U.S. government should engage with developers, including through tech sprints and potentially with research and development grants, to promote innovation that seeks to mitigate the illicit finance risks of DeFi services. Policymakers and regulators should also seek and assess necessary changes in regulation or guidance to support these developments.

Posed Questions

The questions posed below will be considered as part of the recommended actions above, and Treasury welcomes public input on these questions.

- What factors should be considered to determine whether DeFi services are a financial institution under the BSA?

- How can the U.S. government encourage the adoption of measures to mitigate illicit finance risks, such as those identified in Section 5.4 of the report, including by DeFi services that fall outside of the BSA definition of financial institution?

- The assessment finds that non-compliance by covered DeFi services with AML/CFT obligations may be partially attributable to a lack of understanding of how AML/CFT regulations apply to DeFi services. Are there additional recommendations for ways to clarify and remind DeFi services that fall under the BSA definition of a financial institution of their existing AML/CFT regulatory obligations?

- How can the U.S. AML/CFT regulatory framework effectively mitigate the risks of DeFi services that currently fall outside of the BSA definition of a financial institution?

- How should AML/CFT obligations vary based on the different types of services offered by DeFi services?

Annex A

Methodology

This report incorporates published and unpublished research and analysis, insights, and observations of managers and staff from U.S. government agencies. In drafting this assessment, the Treasury's Office of Terrorist Financing and Financial Crimes (TFFC) consulted with staff from the following U.S. government agencies, who also reviewed this report:

- Department of Homeland Security
    - Homeland Security Investigations
    - U.S. Secret Service
- Department of Justice
    - Criminal Division
        - Money Laundering and Asset Recovery Section
        - National Cryptocurrency Enforcement Team
        - Executive Office for U.S. Attorneys
    - Drug Enforcement Administration
    - Federal Bureau of Investigation
    - Virtual Asset Unit
- Department of State
    - Bureau of Economics and Business Affairs
- Department of the Treasury
    - Domestic Finance
    - Internal Revenue Service Criminal Investigations
    - International Affairs
    - Office of Terrorism and Financial Intelligence
        - FinCEN
        - OFAC
        - Office of Intelligence and Analysis
- Staff of the federal functional regulators[134]

---

134   This includes staff of the CFTC, the Office of the Comptroller of the Currency (OCC), and the SEC.

The authors of this report conducted several meetings with U.S. government operational agencies and used open-source reporting from Treasury's risk assessments, open-source reporting from the DOJ, and available court documentation.[135] The risk assessment was also informed by consultations with several U.S. government Departments and Agencies and the over 75 responses to Treasury's Request for Comment, which was issued in conjunction with the publication of the "Action Plan to Mitigate Illicit Finance Risks of Digital Assets"

The terminology and methodology of this risk assessment are based in part on the guidance of the FATF, the international standard-setting body for AML/CFT safeguards. The following concepts are used in this risk assessment:

Threats: For purposes of this assessment, threats are the predicate crimes that are associated with money laundering as well as individuals or entities, or activity undertaken by those individuals and entities, with the potential to cause a defined harm. The environment in which predicate offenses are committed and the proceeds of crime are generated is relevant to understanding why, in some cases, specific crimes are associated with specific money laundering methods.

Vulnerabilities: Vulnerabilities are what facilitate or create the opportunity for misuse of DeFi services to transfer or move funds to launder the proceeds of crime, finance terrorism, or acquire materiel or support revenue generation for WMD programs. They may relate to a specific financial sector or product or a weakness in law, regulation, supervision, or enforcement.

Consequences: Consequences include harms or costs inflicted upon U.S. citizens and the effect on the U.S. economy, which provide further context on the nature of the threats.

Risk: Risk is a function of threat, vulnerability, and consequence. It represents an overall assessment, taking into consideration the effect of mitigating measures including regulation, supervision, and enforcement.

---

135   The charges contained in an indictment are merely allegations. All defendants are presumed innocent unless, and until, proven guilty beyond a reasonable doubt in a court of law.

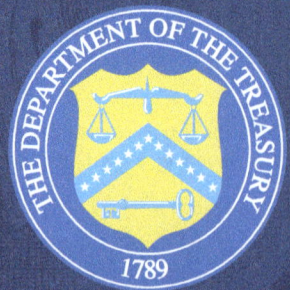

www.ingramcontent.com/pod-product-compliance
Lightning Source LLC
Chambersburg PA
CBHW050501200326

41458CB00014B/5263